Easy A[illegible]
Vocabulary and
Pronunciation

Jane Wightwick and Mahmoud Gaafar

Illustrations by Mahmoud Gaafar

Mc
Graw
Hill
Education

First published 2018 by PALGRAVE.
Published in North America by McGraw-Hill Education.

ISBN: 978-1-260-11763-9 paperback

This book is printed on paper suitable for recycling and made from fully managed and sustained forest sources. Logging, pulping and manufacturing processes are expected to conform to the environmental regulations of the country of origin.

A catalog record for this book is available from the Library of Congress.

Printed and bound in Great Britain by Bell and Bain Ltd, Glasgow

McGraw-Hill Education Language Lab App

Streaming audio recordings are available via app to support your study of this book. Go to www.mhlanguagelab.com to access the online version of the application, or download the free mobile app from the iTunes or Google Play stores.

Note: Internet access required

Contents

www.mhlanguagelab.com

Introduction

Easy Arabic Vocabulary and Pronunciation is a reference and activity book for all beginners and early intermediate students of Arabic.

As a reference book, it provides friendly theme-based vocabulary lists. As an activity book, it helps you to absorb and practise the vocabulary you are learning.

This book assumes you have a reasonable knowledge of the Arabic script and basic grammar.

How to use this book

Each unit of the book is divided into two parts:

- **Part 1**: Core vocabulary, with related activities
- **Part 2**: Extension vocabulary, with related activities.

Part 1 is suitable for early beginners. You can start by working through the core vocabulary and related activities, returning to the extension parts at a later stage.

Part 2 is more suitable for late beginners or early intermediate students. If you are confident of your level, you can complete the core and extension parts together.

The first three units of *Easy Arabic Vocabulary and Pronunciation* focus on basic vocabulary sets and the pronunciation of individual sounds. Subsequent units focus on a particular theme.

The units have a built-in progression. You should feel you are making progress as you move through the book.

Answers to all the activities are included in the final section of the book. You can also find models for the speaking activities on the audio.

Streaming audio

Each copy of *Easy Arabic Vocabulary and Pronunciation* comes with free online audio via the McGraw-Hill Education Language Lab app.

All core and extension vocabulary lists are included in the audio, as are listening activities and models for the end-of-section speaking activities. Those parts of the book which are on the audio are marked with this symbol: . The number under the headphone symbol identifies the audio section online.

Modern Standard Arabic

The vocabulary presented in this book is friendly Modern Standard Arabic which is universally understood in a variety of different situations and will provide you with an excellent base for your written and spoken language.

1 Sounds and basic words 1

Part 1: Core vocabulary

1

Arabic	Pronunciation	English	Write it yourself
أنا	*anā*	I	___
أَنْتَ	*anta*	you *(masc. sing.)*	___
أَنْتِ	*anti*	you *(fem. sing.)*	___
أَنْتُمْ	*antum*	you *(plural)*	___
هُوَ	*huwa*	he	___
هِيَ	*hiya*	she	___
نَحْنُ	*naḥnu*	we	___
هُمْ	*hum*	they *(masc.)*	___
وَ	*wa-*	and	___
هُنا	*huna*	here	___
هُناكَ	*hunāka*	(over) there	___
هَلْ ...؟	*hal ...?*	*question word*	___

2

Pronunciation tip

The letter ح (*ḥā'*)

The letter ح (*ḥā'*) is a breathy 'h' similar to the sound you might make when breathing on glasses to clean them. The letter appears in the list above in the middle of the word for 'we': نَحْنُ (*naḥnu*). It also appears in names of Arabic origin that might be familiar to you. Listen to these names and repeat the Arabic pronunciation carefully.

أَحْمَد *aḥmad* Ahmed — حَمْدي *ḥamdi* Hamdi

سَحَر *saḥar* Sahar — مُحَمَّد *muḥammad* Mohammed

Activity 1

Match the characters with the speech bubbles, as in the example.

١   أحمد

نَحْنُ حَمْدي وَمُحَمَّد.

هَل أَنْتِ سَحَر؟

أَنا أَحْمَد.

مُحَمَّد هُناكَ.

٢   سَحَر

٣   حمدي   محمّد

أَنا سَحَر.

هَل أَنْتَ حَمْدي؟

٤

٥

٦

Activity 2

Write the missing Arabic words in the sentences and questions to match the English translation, as in the example.

I'm Mohammed.	١ ___أَنا___ مُحَمَّد.
She's Sahar.	٢ _____ سَحَر.
Are you Ahmed?	٣ هَل _____ أَحْمَد؟
Are you Sahar?	٤ _____ _____ سَحَر؟
We are here.	٥ _____ هُنا.
Are you (plural) here?	٦ هَل _____ _____؟
Are they over there?	٧ هَل _____ _____؟
I'm Hamdi and he's Ahmed.	٨ _____ حَمْدي وَ _____ أَحْمَد.

Part 2: Extension vocabulary

3

Arabic	Pronunciation	English	Write it yourself
أَنْتُما	*antumā*	you [two] *(dual)*	______
أَنْتُنَّ	*antunna*	you *(fem. plural)*	______
هُما	*humā*	they [two] *(dual)*	______
هُنَّ	*hunna*	they *(fem. plural)*	______
أَهْلاً	*ahlan*	hello	______
مَرْحَباً	*marḥaban*	welcome	______
اِسْمي ...	*ismī ...*	my name's ...	______
تَشَرَّفْنا	*tasharrafnā*	pleased to meet you	______

! Language tip

The ending اً (*-an*)

Some basic Arabic expressions end with a double *fatḥa* vowel sign (ً) pronounced *-an*. This is often written on top of a silent *alif* (اً). Try to remember the spelling and pronunciation of these expressions.

أَهْلاً *ahlan* hello — مَرْحَباً *marḥaban* welcome

شُكْراً *shukran* thank you — أَيْضاً *ayḍan* also

Activity 3

Match the Arabic pronouns to their English equivalents, as in the example.

a she
b they *(fem.)*
c you *(masc. sing.)*
d we
e they *(masc.)*
f they *(dual)*
g you *(fem. pl.)*
h you *(fem. sing.)*
i I
j you *(masc. pl.)*
k he
l you *(dual)*

١ نَحْنُ *d*
٢ هُوَ _
٣ أَنا _
٤ هُنَّ _
٥ أَنْتِ _
٦ أَنْتُما _
٧ أَنْتُنَّ _
٨ أَنْتَ _
٩ هُمْ _
١٠ هُما _
١١ هِيَ _
١٢ أَنْتُمْ _

Activity 4

4 Listen to your audio track. The coach, Captain Mahmoud, is trying to organise his new group of young men and women into teams. Listen and try to decide if the Arabic statements below are true (T) or false (F).

كابتِن مَحْمود: هَلْ أَنْتَ حامِد؟ هَل أَنْتَ سامِح؟

حامِد: أَنا حامِد! سامِح هُناكَ!

كابتِن مَحْمود: أَهْلاً حامِد. هَلْ أَنْتِ سَحَر؟

سَميحة: أَنا سَميحة. أنا اِسْمي سَميحة. وهِيَ سَحَر.

كابتِن مَحْمود: أَهْلاً سَميحة! مَرْحَباً سَحَر! تَشَرَّفْنا!

سَميحة: شُكْراً، كابتِن مَحْمود!

حامِد: نَحْنُ أَيْضاً تَشَرَّفْنا!

١ سامِح هُناكَ. ☐

٢ حامِد هُناك. ☐

٣ سَميحة وسَحَر هُنا. ☐

٤ سَميحة وسَحَر هُناكَ. ☐

٥ الكابتِن اِسْمُهُ أَحْمَد. ☐

٦ الكابتِن اِسْمُهُ مَحْمود. ☐

Language tip

Short vowels

Throughout the first units, we include the short vowel marks – *fatḥa (a), ḍamma (u)* and *kasra (i)*. In subsequent units, we still include the short vowels in the core and extension vocabulary lists, since this is useful for pronunciation. However, we also start to encourage you to recognise words in context without these short vowels, as this is how they will generally appear in Arabic text for native speakers. When writing Arabic yourself, you can include the short vowels or not as you prefer.

2 Sounds and basic words 2

Part 1: Core vocabulary

5

Arabic	Pronunciation	English	Write it yourself
هَذا	*hādhā*	this *(masc.)*	___________
هَذِهِ	*hādhihi*	this *(fem.)*	___________
أَيْنَ؟	*ayna?*	where?	___________
ما؟	*mā?*	what?	___________
مَنْ؟	*man?*	who?	___________
كَبير	*kabīr*	big/large	___________
صَغير	*ṣaghīr*	small	___________
جَديد	*jadīd*	new	___________
قَديم	*qadīm*	old	___________
مَكْسور	*maksūr*	broken	___________
سَليم	*salīm*	unbroken	___________
طَويل	*ṭawīl*	tall/long	___________
قَصير	*qaṣīr*	short	___________

Activity 1

Write هَذا or هَذِهِ in the gaps, as in the example.

١ هَذا بَيْت.

٢ ________ دَرّاجة.

٣ ________ باب.

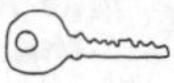
٤ ________ مِفْتاح.

٥ ________ حَقيبة.

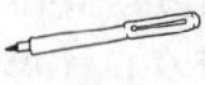
٦ ________ قَلَم.

٧ ________ سَيّارة.

٨ ________ خَيْمة.

6

Pronunciation tip

The emphatic letters

There are four emphatic Arabic letters: ص (*ṣād*), ض (*ḍād*), ط (*ṭā'*) and ظ (*ẓā'*). These letters are pronounced towards the back of the mouth. The sounds differ from their non-emphatic equivalents in much the same way as the initial sounds of the English 'Tim' and 'Tom', or 'silly' and 'sorry', differ. Listen carefully to these pairs of Arabic names. The first name starts with a non-emphatic sound and the second with its emphatic equivalent. Repeat the Arabic pronunciation.

سَميرة *samīra* Samira	تَميم *tamīm* Tamim
صَباح *ṣabāḥ* Sabah	طاهِر *ṭāhir* Tahir
دينا *dīnā* Dina	زَيْد *zayd* Zayd
ضُحَى *ḍuḥā* Duha	ظافِر *ẓāfir* Zafir

7

Activity 2

Sabah is talking to her brother Zayd about the website of a cycling club that she has joined in order to keep fit. Listen and put the transcript of the conversation in the correct order, as in the example.

Additional vocabulary

heroine بَطَلة   woman سَيِّدة   all of them كُلُّها

☐ زيد: بَطَلة كَبيرة؟ ما اِسْمُها؟

☐ صَباح: هَذِهِ بَطَلة كَبيرة في الدَّرّاجات.

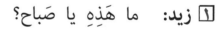

[١] زيد: ما هَذِهِ يا صَباح؟

☐ صَباح: اِسْمُها «كابتِن دينا أَحْمَد».

☐ زيد: ومَنْ هَذِهِ السَّيِّدة الطَّويلة؟

☐ صَباح: هَذِهِ هِيَ الدَّرّاجات الجَديدة.
الدَّرّاجات القَديمة كُلُّها
صَغيرة ومَكْسورة.

Part 2: Extension vocabulary

8

Arabic	Pronunciation	English	Write it yourself
ذَلِكَ	dhālika	that (masc.)	_____
تِلْكَ	tilka	that (fem.)	_____
كَيْفَ؟	kayfa?	how?	_____
ثَقيل	thaqīl	heavy	_____
خَفيف	khafīf	light	_____
سَريع	sarīɛ	fast	_____
جَميل	jamīl	beautiful	_____

💬 Pronunciation tip

Dagger alif
A few Arabic words are written with a *fatḥa* pronounced as a long
ā rather than as a short *a*. Three of these words are in the Unit 2
vocabulary lists: هَذَا *hādhā* ('this' masc.), هَذِهِ *hādhihi* ('this' fem.) and ذَلِكَ
dhālika, ('that' masc.). Another common example is the word for 'but':
لَكِن *lākin*. Pay special attention to the pronunciation of these words.

The traditional spelling is to add a small *alif* mark above the letter
(e.g., هٰذا). This mark is known as a 'dagger *alif*' due to its shape. But
in general a regular *fatḥa* is used in modern Arabic. The most notable
exception is in the spelling of the Arabic word for 'God': الله *allāh*.

Activity 3
Write the missing Arabic question words to match the English translation,
as in the example. Then cover the Arabic and try to write out the complete
questions using the English prompts only.

What's this?	ما هَذا؟	١
Where's the key?	_____ المِفْتاح؟	٢
How are you? ['how's the state?']	_____ الحال؟	٣
Who are they?	_____ هُمْ؟	٤
Is the bag heavy?	_____ الحَقيبة ثَقيلة؟	٥
What's the girl's name?	_____ اِسْم البِنْت؟	٦

Activity 4

Listen to Sabah describing her new racing bicycle, which she has named 'The Feather' (الريشة *ar-rīsha*). First read what she says below, and the additional vocabulary, and decide what type of word might be missing from the gap. Then listen and write in the missing words you hear on your audio track, as in the example.

Additional vocabulary

because لِأَنَّ   like مِثْل   story قِصّة

هٰذه ___ هِيَ دَرّاجَتي الجَديدة.

اِسْمُها "الريشة". _____ لِأَنَّ دَرّاجَتي

سَريعة وَ _____ وَ _____ مِثْل الريشة!

هِيَ قِصّة _____ دَرّاجَتي!

! **Language tip**

Grammatical features of Arabic
Throughout this guide, we are assuming a knowledge of the basic grammatical features of Arabic. These include the feminine ending ة (*-a*), for example دَرّاجة قَديمة *darrāja qadīma* ('an old bicycle'); the possessive endings, for example دَرّاجَتي *darrājatī* ('my bicycle'), and the conjugation of verbs, for example أَشْرَب، يَشْرَب *ashrab, yashrab* ('I drink, he drinks'). You should refer to an Arabic course, for example *Mastering Arabic 1*, and/or a grammar guide, for example *Mastering Arabic Grammar* (published in the U.S. as *Easy Arabic Grammar*) to use alongside this guide.

3 Sounds and basic words 3

Part 1: Core vocabulary

10

Arabic	Pronunciation	English	Write it yourself
فِي	*fī*	in	___________
عَلَى	*ɛala*	on	___________
تَحْتَ	*taḥta*	under	___________
فَوْقَ	*fawqa*	above	___________
بَيْنَ	*bayna*	between	___________
عِنْدَ	*ɛinda*	at/'have'	___________
مِنْ	*min*	from	___________
سَكَنَ/يَسْكُن	*sakana/yaskun*	to live	___________
دَرَسَ/يَدْرُس	*darasa/yadrus*	to study	___________
ذَهَبَ/يَذْهَب	*dhahaba/yadh-hab*	to go	___________
كَتَبَ/يَكْتُب	*kataba/yaktub*	to write	___________
جَلَسَ/يَجْلِس	*jalasa/yajlis*	to sit	___________

11

Pronunciation tip

The letter ع (*ɛayn*)
The guttural sound of the letter ع (*ɛayn*) is particular to Arabic. The letter ع appears in the list above as the initial sound of the word 'at/have', عِنْدَ (*ɛinda*), and 'on', عَلَى (*ɛala*). It also appears as the initial sound of the word 'Arab' itself, عَرَب (*ɛarab*), as well as in the middle of the word for 'yes': نَعَمْ (*naɛam*). Some Arab nationalities also contain this sound. Listen and repeat the Arabic pronunciation carefully.

عِراقيّ *ɛirāqī* Iraqi   عُمانيّ *ɛumānī* Omani   سَعوديّ *saɛūdī* Saudi

Activity 1

Match the speech bubbles to the picture clues, as in the example.

المِفْتاح تَحْتَ الكُرْسيّ.

العُلْبة فَوْقَ المائِدة.

هَذا الجَمَل مِن السَّعوديّة.

كَتَبَتْ سَميحة اِسْمها.

السَّيّارة عِنْدَ الخَيْمة.

مَنْ أَكَلَ السَّمَكة؟

يَجْلِس الكَلْب بَيْنَ الحَقيبَتَيْن.

١

٢

٣

٤

٥

٦

٧

Language tip

الـ (*al-*)

There are a few key points to note when you use الـ *al-* ('the'):

- الـ *al-* is written connected to the front of the word that follows: البَيْت *al-bayt* 'the house'.
- The Arabic alphabet is divided into *sun letters* and *moon letters*. Initial sun letters 'take over' the *l* sound of الـ *al-*. This can be shown with a *shadda* sign (ّ) over the initial letter, for example: الدَّرّاجة *ad-darrāja* 'the bicycle'; السَّمَكة *as-samaka* 'the fish'.
- الـ *al-* will drop the *a* sound if the word before ends with a vowel, for example: في البَيْت *fī l-bayt* 'in the house'. *This only affects the pronunciation and not the spelling.*

Part 2: Extension vocabulary

12

Arabic	Pronunciation	English	Write it yourself
بَعْدَ	*baʕda*	after	________
قَبْلَ	*qabla*	before	________
مَعَ	*maʕa*	with	________
إلى	*ila*	to/towards	________
عَرَفَ/يَعْرِف	*ʕarafa/yaʕrif*	to know	________
سَمِعَ/يَسْمَع	*samiʕa/yasmaʕ*	to hear	________
قالَ/يَقول	*qāla/yaqūl*	to say	________
فَعَلَ/يَفْعَل	*faʕala/yafʕal*	to do	________
رَجَعَ/يَرْجِع	*rajaʕa/yarjiʕ*	to return	________

Activity 2

Match the Arabic verbs to their English equivalents, for example **١b**. Then cover the Arabic and try to write out the verbs using the English prompts only.

a I know	١ نَقول
b we say	٢ تَرْجِع
c you hear *(masc. sing.)*	٣ تَفْعَلين
d he goes	٤ أَعْرِف
e we live	٥ نَجْلِس
f you do *(fem. sing.)*	٦ تَسْمَع
g I study	٧ أَكْتُب
h she returns	٨ يَذْهَب
i we sit	٩ نَسْكُن
j I write	١٠ أَدْرُس

Pronunciation tip

Special ending (*alif maqṣūra*)
A few Arabic words have an ending written with the final shape of the letter *yā'* without the two dots below: ى . This ending is called *alif maqṣūra* ('shortened *alif*') and is pronounced *a*. Two words in the lists opposite have this ending: عَلَى ع*ala* ('on') and إلى ع*ila* ('to/towards').
Alif maqṣūra is also a common ending for feminine Arabic names:

مُنَى *muna* Mona سَلْمَى *salma* Salma
لَيْلَى *layla* Leila هُدَى *huda* Hoda

Activity 3

13

Listen to Salem and Hoda having a chat as they walk in the park and read the transcript below. Then find the Arabic phrases, as in the example.

Additional vocabulary

bridge جِسْر office مَكْتَب university جامِعة

هُدَى: أَنا أَذْهَب إلى الجامِعة بالمِتْرو لِأَنَّني أَسْكُن هُناك،
بَعْدَ الجِسْر.

سالِم: وَماذا تَفْعَلين وَأَنْتِ في المِتْرو؟
هُدَى: أَجْلِس بِجانِب الشُّبّاك،
وأَدْرُس الفَرَنْسِيّة على الهاتِف.
وَأَنْتَ، أَيْنَ تَسْكُن؟
سالِم: نَحْنُ نَسْكُن فَوْقَ مَكْتَب، قَريب مِن الجامِعة.
هُدَى: وَهَل تَذْهَب إلى الجامِعة بالدَّرّاجة؟
سالِم: نَعَمْ، أَذْهَب وَأَرْجِع بِدَرّاجَتي السَّريعة!

١ to the university إلى الجامِعة
٢ by metro ______
٣ after the bridge ______
٤ next to the window ______
٥ on the phone ______
٦ above an office ______
٧ near the university ______
٨ by bike ______
٩ on my fast bike ______

4 The family

Part 1: Core vocabulary

14

Arabic	Pronunciation	English	Write it yourself
عائِلة (ات)	*ɛā'ila (āt)*	family [general]	________
أُسْرة (أُسَر)	*usra (usar)*	family [immediate]	________
أُمّ (أُمَّهات)	*umm (ummahāt)*	mother	________
أَب (آباء)	*ab (ābā')*	father	________
زَوْج (أَزْواج)	*zawj (azwāj)*	husband	________
زَوْجة (ات)	*zawja (āt)*	wife	________
جَدّ (أَجْداد)	*jadd (ajdād)*	grandfather	________
جَدّة (ات)	*jadda (āt)*	grandmother	________
أَخ (إِخْوة)	*akh (ikhwa)*	brother	________
أُخْت (أَخَوات)	*ukht (akhawāt)*	sister	________
اِبْن (أَبْناء)	*ibn (abnā')*	son	________
اِبْنة (بَنات)	*ibna (banāt)*	daughter	________
طِفْل (أَطْفال)	*ṭifl (aṭfāl)*	child	________
مُتَزَوِّج (ون)	*mutazawwij (ūn)*	married	________

! Language tip

Words in the main units (4 to 14) are presented with their plurals in brackets: either ات *āt* / ون *ūn*, or broken plurals spelt out individually. You can hear the singular and plural words on the downloadable audio.

Regular adjectives are shown in the masculine singular; add the ending ة (*-a*) to refer to a female. Other irregular patterns are given separately.

15

Pronunciation tip

The letter خ (*khā'*)
The letter خ (*khā'*) is the sound you might make when clearing your throat, similar to the Scottish pronunciation of the sound 'ch' in 'lo<u>ch</u>'. The letter appears in the Arabic words for 'brother', أَخ (*akh*), and 'sister', أُخْت (*ukht*). It is also the first letter of these Arabic names that might be familiar to you. Listen to the names and repeat the Arabic pronunciation carefully.

خالِد *khālid* Khalid	خُلود *khulūd* Khulud
خَليل *khalīl* Khalil	خَديجة *khadīja* Khadija

Activity 1

Pair the male and female family-related words, for example **١d**.

١ زَوْج	٥ أَب	a اِبْنة	e أُخْت
٢ جَدّ	٦ طِفْل	b أُمّ	f مُتَزَوِّجة
٣ اِبْن	٧ مُتَزَوِّج	c طِفْلة	g جَدّة
٤ أَخ		d زَوْجة	

16

Activity 2

Imagine you are introducing yourself and some of your family, for example:

أَهْلاً. أنا اِسْمي ...	Hello. My name's ...
هَذا أَبي ...	This is my father, ...
وَهَذِهِ أُخْتي ...	And this is my sister, ...

Introduce yourself, and at least two female relatives and two male relatives by name. Practise the introductions out loud. You can listen to the model and then record yourself, getting some feedback from an Arabic speaker if you can. When you are confident, write down your introductions.

Activity 3

Who is who? Khuloud is talking about her family. Read what she says and write the names of her relatives under their pictures on the family tree.

Additional vocabulary   twins تَوْأَمان

اسمي خُلود وأنا مُتَزَوِّجة.

زَوْجي اسمُهُ توم، وهو أَمْريكيّ.

أبي، صالح، مِن بَيْروت وأمّي، خَديجة، مِن عُمان.

عِنْدَنا أربَعة أطفال: ثَلاثة أبناء: خالِد، والتَّوْأمان

سامي ويوسُف؛ وابنة واحِدة اسمُها نورة.

خُلود

! Language tip

Short vowels

High-frequency words and common vocabulary connected to the theme of a unit will sometimes appear within reading activities without short vowels. This is to encourage you to recognise words without the short vowels as this is how they will generally appear in Arabic text for native speakers.

Part 2: Extension vocabulary

17

Arabic	Pronunciation	English	Write it yourself
عَمّ (أَعْمام)	*ɛamm (aɛmām)*	paternal uncle	
عَمّة (ات)	*ɛamma (āt)*	paternal aunt	
خال (أَخْوال)	*khāl (akhwāl)*	maternal uncle	
خالة (ات)	*khāla (āt)*	maternal aunt	
حَم (أَحْماء)	*ḥam (aḥmā')*	father-in-law	
حَماة (حَمَوات)	*ḥamāh (ḥamawāt)*	mother-in-law	
حَفيد (أَحْفاد)	*ḥafīd (aḥfād)*	grandson	
حَفيدة (ات)	*ḥafīda (āt)*	granddaughter	
خَطيب (خُطَباء)	*khaṭīb (khuṭabā')*	fiancé	
خَطيبة (ات)	*khaṭība (āt)*	fiancée	
والِدايَ	*wālidāya*	my parents	
أَعْزَب/عَزْباء	*aɛzab/ɛazbā'*	single [*masc./fem.*]	
مَخْطوب (ون)	*makhtūb (ūn)*	engaged	
مُطَلَّق (ون)	*muṭallaq (ūn)*	divorced	
وُلِدَ/يولَد	*wulida/yūlad*	to be born	
تَزَوَّجَ/يَتَزَوَّج	*tazawwaja/ yatazawwaj*	to get married	

Language tip

Masculine plural ending

The masculine plural ending ون *ūn* can sometimes be written and pronounced as ين *īn*. This depends on how the plural is used in a sentence.

كُلُّهُمْ مُتَزَوِّجون. *kulluhum mutazawwijūn* They are all married.

حَياة المُطَلَّقين صَعبة. *ḥayāt al-muṭallaqīn ṣaɛba.*
The life of divorced people is hard.

Activity 4

Identify the relatives from the description, for example ١c.

١ أُخت أبي هي...
a خالَتي b حَفيدَتي c عَمَّتي

٢ أبو زوجَتي هو...
a عمّي b حَمي c حَماتي

٣ ابن ابنَتي هو...
a حَفيدي b جَدّي c أبي

٤ أُمّ أبي هي...
a عَمَّتي b حَفيدَتي c جَدَّتي

٥ أخو أمّي هو...
a خالي b عَمّي c حَمي

٦ أمّ زوجي هي...
a حَماتي b حَفيدَتي c جَدَّتي

Activity 5

Complete the English sentences to match the Arabic, as in the example.

١ يَسكُن والِدايَ مَعَ جَدَّتي.

My *parents* live with my ________ .

٢ قالَ جدّي إنَّهُ يَذْهَب إلى الحَديقة مَعَ أحفادِه كُلّ يَوْم.

My ________ said that he goes to the park with his ________ every day.

٣ يَعمَل أبناء عَمّتي مَعاً في مَصنَع السَّجّاد.

My ________ work together ________ a carpet factory.

٤ أنا وخَطيبَتي سَنَزور أُسرَتَها في قَريَة "قَصْرالنَّخيل".

My ________ and I will visit her ________ in the village of 'Palace of Palms'.

٥ حَياة عَمَّتي صَعْبة لِأَنّها مُطَلَّقة وأطفالُها صِغار.

The life of my ________ is hard because she is ________ and her ________ are young.

٦ دَفَعَ خالي كُلّ تَكاليف فَرَح أختي الكَبيرة.

My ________ paid all the expenses of the wedding of my older ________.

Language tip

To talk about cousins, nephews, nieces, sisters-in-law or brothers-in-law, you need to be specific about their relationship to you, for example:

اِبن عَمّتي *ibn ʿammatī* the son of my paternal aunt

اِبنة خالي *ibnat khālī* the daughter of my maternal uncle

أُخت زَوْجي *ukht zawjī* the sister of my husband

اِبنة أَخي *ibnat akhī* the daughter of my brother

Activity 6

Ahmad is talking about his family. Read what he says and try to decide if the sentences below are true (T) or false (F). Concentrate on getting the gist of the passage, rather than about understanding every word.

أنا اسمي أحمَد، وزوجتي اسمُها خديجة.

ابنتي الكبيرة اسمُها سامية، وعُمرُها سبع سَنَوات.

إسماعيل عُمرُه أربع سَنَوات، وأميرة عُمرُها ستّة شُهور فَقَط.

وُلِدْتُ هنا، في بَيت أبي الكبير، بِجانِب البَحر.
ولَكِنَّني الآن أسكُن في شَقَّة كَبيرة قَريبة من
مَدرَسة أطفالي. أيّام الجُمعة، نَزور والِدَيَّ
ونَأكُل الغَداء مَعاً. كُلّ عائلتي تُحِبّ البَحر.
هذه صورة خديجة مع ابنة عمّها، شَريفة،
وخطيبها خالد، في الأُسبوع الماضي.

١ أحمد مُتَزَوِّج. ☐

٢ أحمد عِندَه أربعة أطفال. ☐

٣ أسماء أطفاله هي سامية وإسماعيل وأميرة. ☐

٤ أميرة عُمرُها ستّ سَنَوات. ☐

٥ يَسكُن أحمد الآن مَعَ أبيه وأمّه في البيت الكبير. ☐

٦ لا تُحِبّ عائلة أحمد البَحر. ☐

٧ تَزور الأُسرة والِدَيْ أحمد أيّام الجُمعة. ☐

٨ ابنة عمّ خديجة مَخطوبة. ☐

Activity 7

18

Now talk about your own family situation. Use the prompts below and the passage above to help you, adjusting to the feminine if you are female. Write down notes for your description first, and then record yourself. You can listen to the model to review your pronunciation. You can also write up your description using your notes. Show your work to an Arabic speaker if you can.

أنا اِسمي ...	My name's ...
أنا مُتَزَوِّج/أعزَب/مَخطوب/مُطَلَّق	I'm married/single/engaged/divorced
عِنْدي ... أطفال/أبناء/أخَوات، ألخ	I have ... children/sons/sisters, etc.
وُلِدْتُ في ...	I was born in ...
ولكنّي الآن أسكُن في ... مَعَ ...ـي	but now I live in ... with my ...
أيّام الجُمعة/السَّبت/الأَحَد نَزور ...ـي	On Fridays/Saturdays/Sundays, we visit my ...

5 The world of work

Part 1: Core vocabulary

19

Arabic	Pronunciation	English	Write it yourself
مُدَرِّس (ون)	*mudarris (ūn)*	teacher	____________
مُحاسِب (ون)	*muḥāsib (ūn)*	accountant	____________
خَبّاز (ون)	*khabbāz (ūn)*	baker	____________
مُمَرِّض (ون)	*mumarriḍ (ūn)*	nurse	____________
مُهَنْدِس (ون)	*muhandis (ūn)*	engineer	____________
نَجّار (ون)	*najjār (ūn)*	carpenter	____________
طَبّاخ (ون)	*ṭabbākh (ūn)*	cook	____________
مُصَوِّر (ون)	*muṣawwir (ūn)*	photographer	____________
طَبيب (أَطِبّاء)	*ṭabīb (aṭibbā')*	doctor	____________
مُدير (ون)	*mudīr (ūn)*	manager	____________
مُساعِد (ون)	*musāɛid (ūn)*	assistant	____________
مُوَظَّف (ون)	*muwaẓẓaf (ūn)*	employee	____________
عامِل (عُمّال)	*ɛāmil (ɛummāl)*	labourer	____________
فَنّان (ون)	*fannān (ūn)*	artist	____________
عَمَل (أَعْمال)	*ɛamal (aɛmāl)*	work	____________
عَمِلَ/يَعْمَل	*ɛamila/yaɛmal*	to work	____________
مَكْتَب (مَكاتِب)	*maktab (makātib)*	office	____________
مَصْنَع (مَصانع)	*maṣnaɛ (maṣāniɛ)*	factory	____________
مُستَشْفى (مُستَشْفَيات)	*mustashfa (mustashfayāt)*	hospital	____________

Pronunciation tip

Pronouncing double letters (*shadda*)
Many Arabic words for professions contain a double letter sound, for example 'artist' فَنّان (*fannān*), and 'photographer', مُصَوِّر (*muṣawwir*). In written Arabic, the double sound is indicated by a small 'w' sign above the letter called a شَدّة (*shadda*), or 'emphasis', a word which itself appropriately includes the doubling sign. In English, a double letter changes the sound before, for example 'bitter' and 'biter'. However, in Arabic the letter itself needs to be doubled or 'emphasised'. Listen again to the vocabulary list and copy the pronunciation of the *shadda* carefully.

Activity 1

Guess my profession from the equipment I left behind in your apartment, and then write the profession below.

١ ______

٢ ______

٣ ______

٤ ______

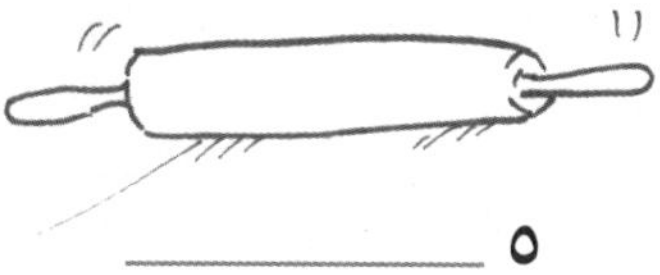

٥ ______

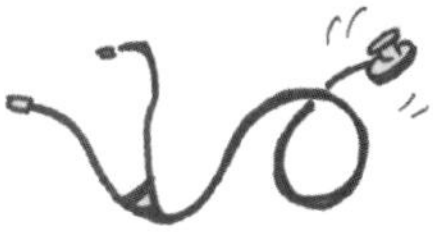

٦ ______

Activity 2

A friend appears always to have issues. Choose the right person to help him.

١ He has chest pains.
a خَبّاز b طَبيب c مُهَنْدِس

٢ He needs a passport photo.
a مُمَرِّضة b طَبّاخ c مُصَوِّر

٣ He wants to learn Chinese.
a مُدَرِّس b نَجّار c مُحاسِب

٤ He wants to mend his cupboard.
a نَجّار b خَبّاز c مُدير

٥ He would like a portrait of his dog.
a طَبّاخ b فَنّان c طَبيب

٦ He has problems with his tax return.
a طَبيب b مُحاسِب c مُصَوِّر

20

Activity 3

Listen to a female broadcaster (مُذيعة *mudhīعa*) interviewing Mohammed, the chief engineer (كبير المُهَندِسين *kabīr al-muhandisīn*). Choose a profession from the list on page 20 to fill the gaps, as in the example. (The professions can be plural so listen carefully.) Then answer the questions below in English.

المُذيعة: هل أنتَ ______مُدير______ هذا المَصنَع الجديد؟

مُحَمَّد: لا. أنا ____________ المُدير،

وكبير الـ__________.

المُذيعة: كَم عَدَد الـ____________

والـ________ هنا؟

مُحَمَّد: نحن أَلْف.

المُذيعة: وما هي ساعات العَمَل هنا؟

مُحَمَّد: نَعمَل ٢٤ ساعة كلّ يوم. بَعض الـ____________

يَسكُنون هناك، وَراء المَصنَع.

المُذيعة: هل أنتَ تَسكُن مَعَهُم، هناك، وَراء المَصنَع؟

مُحَمَّد: لا. أنا أسكُن في قَصر صَغير بِجانِب البَحر.

1 What are Mohammed's two roles in the factory?
2 How many people work in the factory altogether?
3 What hours does the factory operate?
4 Where do some of the factory employees and workers live?
5 Where does Mohammed live?
6 Do you think the factory is near the coast? Why do you think this?

21

Activity 4

Now say something about your own occupation, real or imaginary. Include what you do, where you work and what your hours are. Practise out loud, listening to the model for help with pronunciation. Then write down your passage.

____

____

____

Part 2: Extension vocabulary

22

Arabic	Pronunciation	English	Write it yourself
مَندوب (ون)	*mandūb (ūn)*	representative	___
بَنّاء (ون)	*bannā' (ūn)*	builder	___
مُصَمِّم (ون)	*muṣammim (ūn)*	designer	___
مُحامٍ (مُحامون)	*muḥāmin (muḥāmūn)*	lawyer	___
سائِق (ون)	*sā'iq (ūn)*	driver	___
صُحُفيّ (ون)	*ṣuḥufīy (ūn)*	journalist	___
شَرِكة (ات)	*sharika (āt)*	company	___
وَظيفة (وَظائِف)	*waẓīfa (waẓā'if)*	job	___
راتِب (رَواتِب)	*rātib (rawātib)*	salary	___
مِهْنة (مِهَن)	*mihna (mihan)*	profession	___
اِجْتِماع (ات)	*ijtimāع (āt)*	meeting	___
مَبيعات	*mabīعāt*	sales	___
مَحَلّ (ات)	*maḥall (āt)*	store	___
أدارَ/يُدير	*adāra/yudīr*	to manage	___
ساعَدَ/يُساعِد	*sāعada/yusāعid*	to assist	___
صَنَعَ/يَصْنَع	*ṣanaعa /yaṣnaع*	to manufacture	___

Language tip

Arabic roots

Recognising the three root sounds present in most Arabic words will help you to link related meanings formed from the same root. For example, عامل (*عāmil*), 'worker'/'labourer', and أَعْمَل (*aعmal*), 'I work', from the root ع/م/ل (*ع/m/l*), 'working'; or شَرِكة (*sharika*), 'company', and شَريك (*sharīk*), 'partner', from the root ش/ر/ك (*sh/r/k*), 'sharing'. Mastering the roots and their patterns takes time but gradually you will be able to use them to expand your vocabulary organically.

Activity 5

Ismail is talking about his family's revenue streams. Read what he says, and then decide which of the following sentences are true (T) and which are false (F). (Pay special attention to sentence six because it can be tricky!)

أنا إسماعيل أمين. أعمَل في شَرِكة كبيرة وقَوِيّة،
ولكنّ الرَّواتِب فيها صغيرة وضعيفة. أنا أعمَل في الشَّرِكة
في الصباح، وبَعدَ الظُّهر أعمَل كَسائق تاكسي. أبي، حَسَن
أمين، عِندَهُ تاكسي. يعمَل هو على التاكسي في الصباح،
وبَعدَ الظُّهر يُعطيني المِفتاح. تعمَل زَوْجَتي بَهيجة،
وأُختُها شادية، في مَحَلّ حَماتي لِبَيْع الحَقائب.
رَواتِب المَحَلّ ضعيفة أيضاً، ولكنّها تُساعِدنا.

١ يَعمَل إسماعيل كَسائق تاكسي بَعدَ الظُّهر. ☐

٢ أبو إسماعيل اسمُه أمين حَسَن. ☐

٣ يَعمَل حَسَن كَسائق تاكسي في الصباح. ☐

٤ شادية هي أُخت إسماعيل. ☐

٥ رَواتِب مَحَلّ الحَقائب ضعيفة. ☐

٦ تَعمَل بَهيجة في مَحَلّ أُمِّها. ☐

Activity 6

From what Ismail says, match the Arabic words and expressions below to their English equivalents. Can you say the words correctly without the vowels?

a company	**f** she works	٦ قويّة	١ يعمل
b store	**g** strong	٧ رواتب	٢ ضعيفة
c for selling	**h** driver	٨ تعمل	٣ سائق
d weak/low	**i** salaries	٩ محلّ	٤ أعمل
e I work	**j** he works	١٠ لبيع	٥ شركة

23

Activity 7

Listen to my plans for tomorrow, and fill in the blanks in my calendar.

الخميس، ٢٢ يونيو	
٧:٣٠ ص	اجتماع مع ________
٨:٣٠ ص	اجتماع مع كلّ ________
٢:٠٠ م	زِيارة ________ الجديد
٥:٠٠ م	________ الورد
٦:٠٠ م	زِيارة ________ ________ في ________

24

Activity 8

Now talk about your own family and what they do. Use the prompts below and the vocabulary in this unit to help you. Remember to use the feminine in brackets if appropriate. Write down notes and then record yourself. Play the model to review your pronunciation. You can also write up your description using your notes. Show your work to an Arabic speaker if you can.

...ـي هو (هي) ... My ... is a ...

يَعمَل (تَعمَل) في ... He/she ... works in ...

...ـي هو (هي) مُدير(ة)/مُساعِد(ة)/مُوَظَّف(ة) في ... كبير(ة)/صغير(ة)

My ... is a manager/an assistant/an employee in a large/small ...

...ـي يُدير (تُدير) مَصنَعاً يَصنَع .../مَحَلّاً لِبيع ...

My ... manages a factory which manufactures ... /a store for selling ...

6 Around the house

Part 1: Core vocabulary

25

Arabic	Pronunciation	English	Write it yourself
غُرْفة (غُرَف)	*ghurfa (ghuraf)*	room	______________
شَقّة (شُقَق)	*shaqqa (shuqaq)*	apartment	______________
مائِدة (مَوائِد)	*mā'ida (mawā'id)*	table	______________
كُرْسيّ (كَراسي)	*kursīy (karāsī)*	chair	______________
سَرير (أَسِرّة)	*sarīr (assirra)*	bed	______________
ثَلّاجة (ات)	*thallāja (āt)*	fridge	______________
فُرْن (أَفران)	*furn (afrān)*	oven	______________
خِزانة (ات)	*khizāna (āt)*	cupboard	______________
أَريكة (أَرائِك)	*arīka (arā'ik)*	sofa	______________
سَجّادة (سَجّاد)	*sajjāda/sajjād*	carpet	______________
وِسادة (وَسائِد)	*wisāda (wasā'id)*	pillow/cushion	______________
باب (أَبْواب)	*bāb (abwāb)*	door	______________
شُبّاك (شَبابيك)	*shubbāk (shabābīk)*	window	______________
مَطْبَخ (مَطابِخ)	*maṭbakh (maṭābikh)*	kitchen	______________
حَمّام (ات)	*ḥammām (āt)*	bathroom	______________
غُرْفة نَوْم (غُرَف نَوْم)	*ghurfat nawm (ghuraf nawm)*	bedroom	______________
حَديقة (حَدائِق)	*ḥadīqa (ḥadā'iq)*	garden	______________
(لَيْسَ) هُناكَ ...	*(laysa) hunāka …*	there is (not)/ are (not)	______________

26

Pronunciation tip

The letter غ (*ghayn*)

The sound represented by the letter غ (*ghayn*) is pronounced at the back of the throat as if gargling, similar to the French pronunciation of 'rue'. It is the first letter of the Arabic word for 'room', غُرْفة (*ghurfa*), and the middle letter of the word for 'small', صَغير (*ṣaghīr*). It is also the first letter of these Arabic names. Listen and repeat the pronunciation carefully.

غالِب *ghālib* Ghalib — غادة *ghāda* Ghada

غَيْث *ghayth* Ghaith — غالِية *ghāliya* Ghalya

Activity 1

In Arabic, write the name of the object each man is carrying.

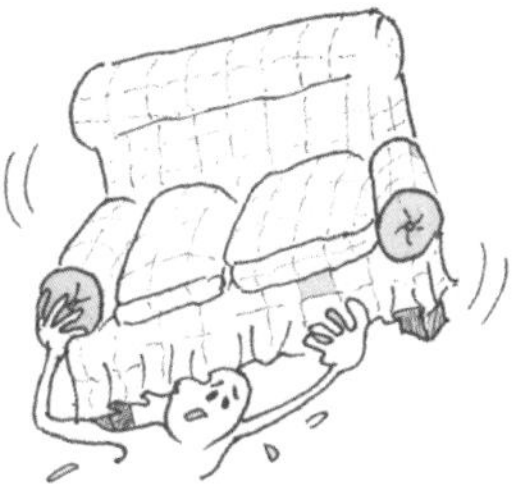

١ ______

٢ ______

٣ ______

٤ ______

٥ ______

٦ ______

Activity 2

Match the phrases with their opposites, for example ١e.

١	على السرير	a	الخِزانة الصغيرة
٢	بِجانِب باب الحَمّام	b	لَيْسَ هناك وَسائد
٣	أمام الشبّاك	c	الثلّاجة هناك
٤	الخِزانة الكبيرة	d	بَعيد عَن باب الحَمّام
٥	الثلّاجة هنا	e	تَحتَ السرير
٦	هناك وَسائد	f	وَراء الشبّاك

Activity 3

Geraldine McMurphy is moving house in Cairo, but she doesn't speak Arabic. She's given you these instructions about where she wants her furniture. Write them out in Arabic for the removal men. The first instruction has been started for you.

١ the small bed in the small room

السرير الصغير في ______

٢ the big cupboard beside the sofa

______

٣ the fridge beside kitchen door ('door of the kitchen')

______

٤ the big bed and the chairs in the bedroom

______

٥ all the pillows on the big bed

______

٦ the oven between the window and the door

______

Activity 4

27

Give a basic description of your home. Use these prompts to help you:

أسكُن في بَيْت كبير/شَقّة صغيرة	I live in a large house/a small apartment
هناك غُرفَتان/ثَلاث غُرَف، إلخ	There are two rooms/three rooms, etc.
في غُرفَتي/في المَطبَخ هناك ...	In my room/in the kitchen, there is/are ...
ولكن لَيْسَ هناك ...	But there isn't/aren't ...

Practise out loud, listening to the model for help with pronunciation. You can record yourself if you want to review yourself, and get some feedback from an Arabic speaker. When you are confident, write down your description.

______

______

______

______

Part 2: Extension vocabulary

28

Arabic	Pronunciation	English	Write it yourself
شُرْفة (ات)	*shurfa (āt)*	balcony	________
غُرْفة مَعيشة (غُرَف مَعيشة)	*ghurfat maɛīsha (ghuraf maɛīsha)*	living room	________
حَمّام سِباحة (حَمّامات سِباحة)	*ḥammām sibāḥa (ḥammāmāt sibāḥa)*	swimming pool	________
سَقْف (أَسْقُف)	*saqf (asquf)*	ceiling	________
سَطْح (أَسْطُح)	*saṭḥ (asṭuḥ)*	roof	________
سُلَّم (سَلالِم)	*sullam (salālim)*	stairs	________
مِصْعَد (مَصاعِد)	*miṣɛad (maṣāɛid)*	elevator	________
طابِق (طَوابِق)	*ṭābiq (ṭawābiq)*	storey/floor	________
سِتار (سَتائِر)	*sitār/satā'ir*	curtain	________
مُكَيِّف الهَواء	*mukayyif al-hawā'*	air conditioner	________
غَسّالة (ات)	*ghassāla (āt)*	washing machine	________
سُفْرة (ات)	*sufra (āt)*	dining table	________
حَديث	*ḥadīth*	modern	________
تَقْليديّ	*taqlīdī*	traditional	________
فاخِر	*fākhir*	luxurious	________
مُريح	*murīḥ*	comfortable	________
واسِع	*wāsiɛ*	spacious	________
مَفْروش	*mafrūsh*	furnished	________
تَكَوَّنَ/يَتَكَوَّن مِن	*takawwana/ yatakawwan min*	to consist of	________
اِسْتَأْجَرَ/يَسْتَأْجِر	*ista'jara/yasta'jir*	to rent	________

Activity 5

Match the positions in the box to the picture clues, for example ١f.

١ فوق الغسّالة
٢ في المطبخ
٣ تحت السجّادة
٤ أمام المصعد
٥ بجانب حمّام السباحة
٦ على السلّم
٧ وراء الستار

a

b

c

d

e

f

g

Activity 6

Ghalib is describing his life on the road. Read what he says, and then decide which of the sentences on page 31 is true (T) and which is false (F).

أنا اسمي غالب. أنا مَندوب مَبيعات في المَمْلَكة العَرَبيّة السَّعوديّة. أَنْتَقِل من مدينة إلى مدينة، ومن فُندُق إلى فُندُق. أمس، كُنتُ في الرِّياض. كانَتْ غُرفَتي في الفُندُق الفاخِر هناك مِثل غُرفَتي هنا، اليوم. ولكنَّني اليوم في الدَّمام. غَداً، سَأطير إلى أبْها، وسَتَكون غُرفَتي في الفُندُق هناك مِثل غُرفَتي اليوم، وغُرفة الأمس. سَتَكون هناك كَراسي مُريحة، ومائدة كبيرة وثلّاجة صغيرة. مُكَيِّف الهَواء سَيَكون فوق الباب، وسَتَكون هناك خزانة واسعة فيها وِسادة سابِعة، لِأن هناك ستّ وَسائد على السرير الكبير.

1 Ghalib is a travelling sales rep. ☐

2 Today, Ghalib is in Dammam. ☐

3 Tomorrow, Ghalib flies to Riyadh. ☐

4 Ghalib thinks all hotel rooms look the same. ☐

5 Ghalib will take a train to Abha. ☐

6 There will be a total of six pillows in the room tomorrow. ☐

Activity 7

Now find the Arabic phrases below in what Ghalib says, as in the example.

١ I'll fly to Abha
سأطير إلى أبها

٢ the luxury hotel
____

٣ I move from town to town
____

٤ a sales representative
____

٥ a seventh pillow
____

٦ comfortable chairs
____

٧ above the door
____

٨ a small fridge
____

Activity 8

29

Now describe your own apartment or house. Use the prompts below to get you started, but try to include as much detail of the furniture as you can including size, age, comfort, etc. Write down notes and then record yourself. Play the model to review your pronunciation. You can also write up your description using your notes. Show your work to an Arabic speaker if you can.

يَتَكَوَّن بَيْتنا من ... غُرَف، وهي: Our house consists of ... rooms which are:

نَسْتَأْجِر شَقَّتنا. شَقَّتنا في الطابِق الـ... . هناك/لَيْسَ هناك مِصْعَد.

We rent our apartment. Our apartment is on the ... floor. There is/there isn't a lift

المَطْبَخ/الحَمّام حَديث/تَقْليديّ/واسِع/فاخِر

The kitchen/bathroom is modern/traditional/spacious/luxurious

في غُرْفَة المَعيشة هناك/لَيْسَ هناك ...

In the living room there is (are)/there isn't (aren't) ...

7 Around town

Part 1: Core vocabulary

30

Arabic	Pronunciation	English	Write it yourself
مَدينة (مُدُن)	*madīna (mudun)*	town/city	__________
جامِعة (ات)	*jāmiɛa (āt)*	university	__________
مَدْرَسة (مَدارِس)	*madrasa (madāris)*	school	__________
شارِع (شَوارِع)	*shāriɛ (shawāriɛ)*	street	__________
جِسْر (جُسور)	*jisr (jusūr)*	bridge	__________
سوق (أَسْواق)	*sūq (asāq)*	market	__________
مَحَطّة (ات)	*maḥaṭṭa (āt)*	station	__________
مَوْقِف (مَواقِف)	*mawqif (mawāqif)*	[bus] stop	__________
مَطْعَم (مَطاعِم)	*maṭɛam (maṭāɛim)*	restaurant	__________
مَسْجِد (مَساجِد)	*masjid (masājid)*	mosque	__________
مَطار (ات)	*maṭār (āt)*	airport	__________
فُنْدُق (فَنادِق)	*funduq (fanādiq)*	hotel	__________
يَمين	*yamīn*	right	__________
يَسار	*yasār*	left	__________
وَسَط المَدينة	*wasaṭ al-madīna*	city centre	__________
نَزَلَ/يَنْزِل	*nazala/yanzil*	to get off/alight	__________
أَخَذَ/يَأْخُذ	*akhadha/ya'khudh*	to take	__________
رَكِبَ/ يَرْكَب	*rakiba/yarkab*	to ride	__________

31

Pronunciation tip

The letter ق (*qāf*)

The sound of the letter ق (*qāf*) is similar to an English 'q' sound but produced further back in the throat, as if you are blowing a bubble at the back of your throat while saying 'q'. The word for market (or 'souk') ends with the letter ق (*qāf*): سوق *sūq*. It is also one of the letters in these Arab place names. Listen and repeat the Arabic pronunciation carefully.

قَطَر *qaṭar* Qatar — العِراق *al-irāq* Iraq

القاهِرة *al-qāhira* Cairo — مَسْقَط *musqaṭ* Muscat

Activity 1

Match the English and the Arabic directions, for example ١c.

Go to the train station. **a**	١ خُذْ أَوَّل شارِع على اليَمين.
How do I get to the centre of Muscat? **b**	٢ اِرْكَبي الباص إلى الجِسر.
Take the first street on the right. **c**	٣ أَيْنَ شارِع السوق؟
Get off at the university. **d**	٤ اِذْهَبي إلى مَحَطّة القِطار.
Where's Market Street? **e**	٥ وَسَط مَدينة مَسْقَط مِنْ أَيْنَ؟
Ride the bus to the bridge. **f**	٦ اِنْزِل عِنْدَ الجامِعة.

Activity 2

32 Choose three places around town from the list. Ask for directions and give a response, using the phrases below. Practise out loud, listening to the model for help with pronunciation. You can record yourself and get some feedback from an Arabic speaker. When you are confident, write down your directions.

أَيْنَ ...؟/ ... مِنْ أَيْنَ؟ Where's .../How do I get to ...?

اِذْهَبْ، اِذْهَبي إلى ... Go *(masc., fem.)* to ...

خُذْ، خُذي/ اِرْكَبْ، اِرْكَبي ... Take *(masc., fem.)*/Ride *(masc., fem.)* ...

اِنْزِلْ، اِنْزِلي عِنْدَ ... Get off *(masc., fem.)* at ...

Activity 3

These characters are looking for work. Guide them to their most promising destinations.

Additional vocabulary

post office مَكْتَب البَريد

١ أنتَ مُدَرِّس؟ اِذْهَب إلى ...
a المَدرَسة b الجِسر c الفُندُق

٢ أنتَ طَبّاخ؟ اِذْهَب إلى ...
a الجامِعة b المَحَطّة c المَطعَم

٣ أنتِ مُمَرِّضة؟ اِذْهَبي إلى...
a المَطار b المُستَشفى
c مَكتَب البَريد

٤ أنتَ سائِق قِطار؟ اِذْهَب إلى ...
a المَحَطّة b الشارِع c الفُندُق

٥ أنتُم مُوَظَّفون؟ اِذْهَبوا إلى ...
a الفُندُق b الجِسر c الشارِع

٦ أنتِ مُحاسِبة؟ اِذْهَبي إلى ...
a المَطعَم b المُستَشفى
c البَنك

Activity 4

33 Hakim is talking about his daily working routine. First listen to what he says and write the missing words, as in the example.

أنا اسمي حكيم. أنا سائِق باص. أنا أعرِف كلّ شارع
في هذه المدينة الجميلة، وكلّ ______،
وكلّ بيت. في الصباح، يركَب بَعض الناس الباص،
وهو في ______، قَبلَ أن أَخرُج بِهِ
إلى الشوارع. بَعدَ أن نَخرُج من
______ المدينة، وبَعدَ ______
الكبير، آخُذ طريق الملك حتّى
مَوقِف ______. ينزل الطَّلَبة
والمُدَرِّسون هناك. بعد ذلك، آخُذ أوّل
شارع على ______، لِآخُذ ______
المطار إلى محطّة ______، محطّة المُمَرِّضات والمُمَرِّضين!
يَقول كلّ الناس: «______ يا عمّ حكيم!» وأنا أقول لَهُمْ،
«مع السلامة يا أَصْدِقائي!»، ثُمَّ ______ بالباص حتّى المطار.

Activity 5

A local magazine is doing a feature on Hakim. Help them by deciding if the statements below about Hakim and his bus route are true (T) or false (F).

١ حكيم هو سائِق باص في المدينة. ☐

٢ هناك جامِعة في المدينة. ☐

٣ المُستَشفى على طَريق المَطار. ☐

٤ يذهَب حكيم إلى الجِسر الكبير قبلَ أن يخرُج من وَسَط المدينة. ☐

٥ يأخُذ حكيم أوّل شارع على اليَسار بعد المُستَشفى. ☐

٦ كلّ الناس يَعرِفون حكيم. ☐

Part 2: Extension vocabulary

34

Arabic	Pronunciation	English	Write it yourself
عاصِمة (عَواصِم)	*ع‍āṣima (ع‍awāṣim)*	capital	________
مَيْدان (مَيادين)	*maydān (mayādīn)*	roundabout/ square	________
قَريب، أَقْرَب	*qarīb, aqrab*	near, nearest	________
طَريق (طُرُق)	*ṭarīq (ṭuruq)*	road	________
قِسْم الشُّرْطة (أَقْسام الشُّرْطة)	*qism ash-shurṭa (aqsām ash-shurṭa)*	police station	________
رَصيف (أَرْصِفة)	*raṣīf (arṣifa)*	pavement	________
ناصية (نَواصٍ)	*nāṣya (nawāṣin)*	street corner	________
عِمارة (ات)	*ع‍imāra (āt)*	apartment block	________
إشارة (ات) مُرور	*ishārat (āt) murūr*	traffic light	________
مَشَى/يَمْشي	*masha/yamshī*	to walk	________
سَأَلَ/يَسْأَل	*sa'ala/yas'al*	to ask	________
(لا) يوجَد، (لا) توجَد	*(lā) yūjad, (lā) tūjad*	can(not) be found	________

Activity 6

Read the story about Khadija and her search for a specific local restaurant. Fill in the blanks in the English summary below, as in the example.

نَزَلَتْ خديجة بَرَكات من غُرفَتِها الفاخِرة في فندق «قَصر النُّجوم»، وسَألَتْ عامِل المِصعَد الشابّ: "أين مَطعَم الفَنّانين من فضلك؟". قالَ العامِل: "آسِف. أنا لا أعرِف. أنا لا أسكُن هنا. اِسألي في مكتب البريد. المكتب قَريب جِدّاً من الفندق. أوّل شارع على اليَسار، قبلَ المَيدان."

دَخَلَتْ خديجة بَرَكات مكتب البريد، وسَألَت المُوَظَّف: "أين مَطعَم الفَنّانين من فضلك؟". قالَ المُوَظَّف: "مَطعَم الفَنّانين؟ أنا سَمِعْتُ هذا الاسم، ولكن لا أعرِف في أيّ شارع. اِسألي في قِسم الشُّرطة. القِسم بجانب هذا المكتب على نَفس الرَّصيف، عند إشارة المُرور."

مَشَتْ خديجة على الرَّصيف نَحوَ إشارة المُرور، ثُمَّ دَخَلَتْ قِسم الشُّرطة، وقالَتْ للشُّرطيّ: "أين مَطعَم الفَنّانين من فضلك؟". قالَ الشُّرطيّ: "آسِف يا ابنَتي. لا أعرِف هذا المَطعَم. اِسألي في فندق «قَصر النُّجوم». عامل المِصعَد هناك ابن أُختي. هو سَيَعرِف!"

1 *Khadija* Barakat was looking for *The Artists'* __________.

2 She was staying in a __________ called __________ *of the* __________.

3 First, she __________ the boy who operates the __________.

4 He suggested asking at the __________ office. 'Take the __________ street on the __________', he said, '__________ the square.'

5 So, next Khadija __________ the __________ at the __________ __________, and he __________ __________ either.

6 By the __________ of the story, Khadija had gone a complete __________!

Activity 7

Now choose the best answers for the questions about Khadija's story.

١ مَن هي والِدة عامل المِصعَد؟

a أُخت خديجة **b** والِدة خديجة **c** أُخت الشُّرطيّ

٢ أين تسكُن خديجة بَرَكات وهي في هذه المدينة؟

a في فندق الفَنّانين **b** في فندق قَصر النُّجوم **c** في عِمارة النُّجوم

٣ إلى أين مَشَتْ خديجة بعدَ مكتب البَريد؟

a إلى الفندق **b** إلى إشارة المُرور **c** إلى أوّل شارع على اليَسار

٤ هل مكتب البَريد وقِسم الشُّرطة على رَصيف واحد؟

a لا **b** لا نعرِف **c** نعم

٥ كيف يعرِف عامل المِصعَد الشُّرطيّ؟

a يَعمَل الشُّرطيّ في الفندق **b** الشُّرطيّ هو خالُه

c عامل المِصعَد هو ابن الشُّرطيّ وخديجة

> **Language tip**
>
> **The town 'square'**
>
> The Arabic word مَيْدان *maydān* is often translated into English as 'square' in the context of a town or city, for example مَيْدان التَّحْرير *maydān at-taḥrīr*, 'Tahrir Square'. In reality the *maydān* is just as likely to be round as square. The word originates from 'ground' or 'battlefield', and has no connection to the shape of the feature.

Activity 8

35 Now talk about your home town. Use the prompts below to help you. Write down notes for your description first, and then record yourself. Play the model to review your pronunciation. You can also write up your description using your notes. Show your work to an Arabic speaker if you can.

أنا أَسْكُن في ... I live in ...

بَيْتي/عِمارَتي بِجانِب/أَمامَ/قَريب(ة) مِن ... My house/block is next to/in front of/near ...

في مَدينَتي يوجَد/توجَد ... In my town ... can be found

ولكن لا يوجَد/لا توجَد ... But ... can't be found

آخُذ الـ... إلى المَكتَب/المَدرَسة/الجامِعة I take the ... to the office/school/university

أَيّام الجُمعة/السَّبت/الأَحَد أذهب إلى ... On Fridays/Saturdays/Sundays, I go to ...

8 The world of education

Part 1: Core vocabulary

36

Arabic	Pronunciation	English	Write it yourself
طالِب (طُلّاب)	*ṭālib (ṭullāb)*	student	______
تِلْميذ (تَلاميذ)	*tilmīdh (talāmīdh)*	pupil	______
مُعَلِّم (ون)	*muعallim (ūn)*	instructor, teacher	______
دَرْس (دُروس)	*dars (durūs)*	lesson	______
مَكْتَبة (ات)	*maktaba (āt)*	library	______
صَفّ (صُفوف)	*ṣaff (ṣufūf)*	class, grade	______
اِمْتِحان (ات)	*imtiḥān (āt)*	exam	______
لُغة (ات)	*lugha (āt)*	language	______
عِلْم (عُلوم)	*عilm (عulūm)*	science	______
الرِّياضيّات	*ar-riyāḍiyyāt*	mathematics	______
التاريخ	*at-tārīkh*	history	______
الجُغْرافِيا	*al-jughrāfiyā*	geography	______
الرِّياضة	*ar-riyāḍa*	sport	______
الموسيقَى	*al-mūsīqa*	music	______
الرَّسْم	*ar-rasm*	art/drawing	______
التَّرْبِية الدينيّة	*at-tarbiya ad-dīnīyya*	religious education	______
قَرَأ/يَقْرَأ	*qara'a/yaqra'*	to read	______
تَعَلَّمَ/يَتَعَلَّم	*taعallama/ yataعallam*	to learn	______

Language tip

Additional vocabulary relevant to the world of education has been presented in previous units. For example, in Unit 3 you will find the verbs 'to study' دَرَسَ/يَدْرُس (*darasa/yadrus*) and 'to write' كَتَبَ/يَكْتُب (*kataba/yaktub*). In Unit 5 you will find the word for 'teacher' مُدَرِّس (*mudarris*), and in Unit 7 the words for 'school' مَدْرَسة (*madrasa*) and 'university' جامِعة (*jāmiʿa*). This overlap of vocabulary themes occurs frequently, and it is always a good idea to review previous lists for relevant words.

Activity 1

Match the school subjects in the box to the picture clues, for example ١f.

١ الرِّياضة	٤ الموسيقى	٧ العُلوم
٢ الرَّسْم	٥ القِراءة	٨ اللُّغات
٣ الجُغْرافِيا	٦ الرِّياضيّات	٩ التاريخ

c

b

a

f

e

d

i

h

g

Activity 2

Read these highlights from your weekly schedule, then answer the Arabic questions below, as in the example.

جغرافيا	٨،٣٠ صباحاً	الثُّلاثاء
موسيقى	٢،٠٠ بعد الظُّهر	الإِثْنَيْن
رسم	٨،٣٠ صباحاً	السَّبْت
تاريخ	٩،١٥ صباحاً	الأَرْبِعاء
رياضيّات	١،٣٠ بعد الظُّهر	الأَحَد
علوم	١٠،١٥ صباحاً	الخَميس
لغة فَرَنسيّة	٩،٣٠ صباحاً	الجُمْعة

١ في أيّ يَوْم تَدرُسون الموسيقى؟ يوم الاثنين

٢ في أيّ ساعة تَدرُسون الفَرَنسيّة؟ ______

٣ في أيّ يَوْم تَدرُسون الرسم؟ ______

٤ في أيّ ساعة تَدرُسون العلوم؟ ______

٥ في أيّ يَوْم تَدرُسون الجغرافيا؟ ______

٦ في أيّ ساعة تَدرُسون الرياضيّات؟ ______

37

Activity 3

Say something about your own education. Use these prompts to help you:

أنا كُنْتُ تِلميذاً (تِلميذة) في مَدْرَسة ... I was a pupil at (a) ... school

أنا طالِب (طالِبة) في جامِعة ... I am a student at (a) ... university

(كُنْتُ) أَدْرُس ... يَوْم الـ... I (used to) study ... on ... day

(كُنْتُ) أُحِبّ ... I (used to) like ...

(لا) أُجيد ... I am (not) good at ...

Practise out loud, listening to the model for help with pronunciation. When you are confident, write down your description.

______

______

______

______

Part 2: Extension vocabulary

38

Arabic	Pronunciation	English	Write it yourself
التَّعْليم/التَّرْبِية	*at-taɛlīm/at-tarbiya*	education	______________
كُلّيّة (ات)	*kulliyya (āt)*	college, faculty	______________
مُحاضَرة (ات)	*muḥāḍara (āt)*	lecture	______________
أُسْتاذ (أَساتِذة)	*ustādh (asātidha)*	professor, lecturer	______________
دَوْرة (ات)	*dawra (āt)*	course	______________
مادّة (مَوادّ)	*mādda (mawādd)*	subject	______________
الهَنْدَسة	*al-handasa*	engineering	______________
الطِّبّ	*aṭ-ṭibb*	[study of] medicine	______________
الحُقوق	*al-ḥuqūq*	[study of] law	______________
رَوْضة (رِياض)	*rawḍa (riyāḍ)*	kindergarten	______________
اِبْتِدائيّ	*ibtidā'ī*	primary	______________
إعْداديّ	*iɛdādī*	preparatory	______________
ثانويّ	*thānawī*	secondary	______________
دَرَّسَ/يُدَرِّس	*darrasa/yudarris*	to teach	______________
عَلِمَ/يَعْلَم	*ɛalima/yaɛlam*	to know (a fact)	______________
عَلَّمَ/يُعَلِّم	*ɛallama/yuɛallim*	to instruct	______________
سَجَّلَ/يُسَجِّل	*sajjala/yusajjil*	to enrol	______________

Cultural tip

Schools in the Arab World are often divided into three core levels: اِبْتِدائيّ (*ibtidā'ī*) 'primary' or 'elementary' (ages 5–11); إعْداديّ (*iɛdādī*) 'preparatory' (ages 12–14), also known as مُتَوَسِّط (*mutawassiṭ*) 'middle'; and ثانويّ (*thānawī*) 'secondary' (ages 15–17). University courses are usually four years and students can be as young as 17 when they start.

Activity 4

Write the missing Arabic words in the sentences to match the English translation, as in the example.

I am a student at secondary school.	١ أنا طالب في المدرسة الثانوية.
I left middle school last year.	٢ غادَرْتُ المدرسة ________ السَّنة ________.
I like Mondays.	٣ أنا ________ أيّام ________.
We study science in the morning.	٤ نحن ________ العُلوم في ________.
Majid prefers Tuesdays.	٥ ________ ماجد ________ الثُّلاثاء.
He likes reading history books.	٦ ________ أن ________ كُتُب ________.
I'd like to enrol my daughter in the faculty of medicine.	٧ ________ أن ________ اِبْنَتي في كُلّيّة ________.
Majid hopes to enrol [himself] in the faculty of law.	٨ يأمَل ________ أن ________ نَفسَهُ في ________ الحُقوق.

Activity 5

Ibrahim is talking about his son, Faris. Read what he says, and then find the Arabic to match the English phrases at the top of page 43, as in the example.

أُريد أن أُسَجِّل ابني فارس لِيدرُس في كُلّيّة الهَندَسة بجامعة «وارسو» في بولندا. أُريد من الأَساتِذة هناك أن يُعَلِّموه كيف تُصنَع الغَسّالات أو الثَّلّاجات. أُريده أن يَتَعَلَّم كيف تعمَل المَصاعِد ومُكَيِّفات الهَواء في الأَبنِيَة الكبيرة. وبعد أن يرجِع إلَيْنا وهو مُهندس كبير ومُهِمّ، سَيجِد عَمَلاً بسُرعة وبسُهولة في أيّ مَصنَع أو فُندُق هنا في مَدينَتِنا أو في أيّ مدينة قريبة. أو، رُبَّما، يعمَل كأُستاذ هنا ويُدَرِّس الهَندَسة لِأبناء البَلَد!

١ the faculty of engineering

كلّيّة الهندسة

٢ Warsaw University

____

٣ the professors/the lecturers

____

٤ how washing machines are made

____

٥ how elevators work

____

٦ a big and important engineer

____

٧ quickly and easily

____

٨ the youngsters in our country

____

Activity 6

Now read what Ibrahim says again and decide if the following sentences are true (T) or false (F).

1 Ibrahim wants his son, Faris, to study medicine. ☐

2 He hopes his son will be able to study in Poland. ☐

3 He wants him to learn practical skills. ☐

4 He hopes that Faris will stay and work in Poland after his studies. ☐

5 Ibrahim thinks his son will find work easily if he returns. ☐

6 He believes his son will maybe in turn teach the next generation. ☐

Activity 7

39

Describe your education and/or aspirations in detail. Use the prompts below and the vocabulary in this unit to get you started. Play the model to review your pronunciation. Write down notes and then record yourself, or present to a group. You can also write up your description using your notes. Show your work to an Arabic speaker if you can.

ما زِلْتُ في المدرسة/الكُلّيّة/الجامعة. I am still at school/college/university.

غادَرْتُ المدرسة/الكُلّيّة/الجامعة مُنْذُ ... I left school/college/university ... ago.

(كانَتْ) المَوادّ المُفَضَّلة عِندي في المدرسة/الكُلّيّة/الجامعة ...

My favourite subjects at school/college/univerity are (were) ...

أَدْرُس/دَرَسْتُ/أُريد أن أَدْرُس ... I am studying/studied/would like to study ...

أَعْتَقِد أنَّ المُحاضرات/الدَّوْرة/الدُّروس (كانَتْ) ... جِدّاً.

I think the lectures/the course/the lessons are (were) very ...

9 The Arab World

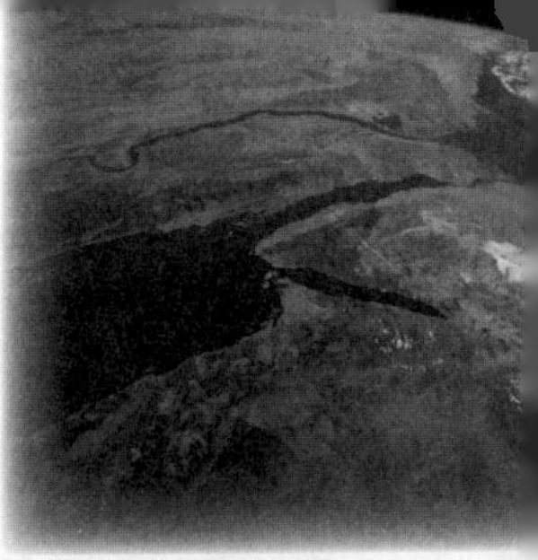

Part 1: Core vocabulary

40

Arabic	Pronunciation	English	Write it yourself
الشَّرْق الأَوْسَط	*ash-sharq al-awsaṭ*	The Middle East	______
مِصْر/مِصْريّ	*miṣr/miṣrīy*	Egypt/Egyptian	______
لُبْنان/لُبْنانيّ	*lubnān/lubnānīy*	Lebanon/ Lebanese	______
سورِيا/سوريّ	*sūriyā/sūrīy*	Syria/Syrian	______
العِراق/عِراقيّ	*al-ɛirāq/ɛirāqīy*	Iraq/Iraqi	______
السَّعوديّة/سَعوديّ	*as-saɛūdīyya/ saɛūdīy*	Saudi [Arabia]/ Saudi	______
الأُرْدُنّ/أُرْدُنّيّ	*al-urdunn/ urdunnīy*	Jordan/ Jordanian	______
أَمْريكا/أَمْريكيّ	*amrīkā/amrīkīy*	America/ American	______
بِريطانْيا/بِريطانيّ	*biriṭānyā/biriṭānīy*	Britain/British	______
بَلَد (بِلاد)	*balad (bilād)*	country	______
عاصِمة (عَواصِم)	*ɛāṣima (ɛawāṣim)*	capital	______
شَمال	*shamāl*	north	______
جَنوب	*janūb*	south	______
شَرْق	*sharq*	east	______
غَرْب	*gharb*	west	______
سافَرَ/يُسافِر	*sāfara/yusāfir*	to travel	______
زارَ/يَزور	*zāra/yazūr*	to visit	______
نَزَلَ/يَنْزِل	*nazala/yanzil*	to stay *(at a hotel, etc.)*	______

41

Language tip

Countries and nationalities

You can see a pattern in the Arab countries and nationalities, with the country name often starting with *al-* ('the'), and the nationality ending with the sound *-īy*. Here are some more Arab countries and nationalities that will immediately sound familiar to you. Listen and repeat the Arabic pronunciation.

قَطَر *qaṭar* Qatar

قَطَريّ *qaṭarīy* Qatari

الكُوَيْت *al-kuwayt* Kuwait

كُوَيْتيّ *kuwaytīy* Kuwaiti

البَحْرَيْن *al-baḥrayn* Bahrain

بَحْرَيْنيّ *baḥraynīy* Bahraini

الإمارات *al-imārāt* The Emirates

إماراتيّ *imārātīy* Emirati

Activity 1

Each of the following has a specific purpose for travel. Match the purpose to the appropriate destination.

١ I want to visit Baghdad.

a السعوديّة b سوريا c العراق

٢ I want to visit the Pyramids.

a لبنان b بريطانيا c مصر

٣ I want to visit Mecca and Medina.

a السعوديّة b قطر c أمريكا

٤ I want to visit Abu Dhabi and Dubai.

a الأردنّ b الإمارات c لبنان

٥ I want to visit Buckingham Palace.

a أمريكا b البحرين c بريطانيا

٦ I want to visit Hollywood.

a مصر b أمريكا c الكويت

42

Activity 2

Say where you are from and where you have travelled. Use the prompts below to help you. Don't forget to listen to the model for help with pronunciation and to record yourself. When you are confident, write down what you said.

أنا مِن ... I'm from ...

(السَّنة الماضية/مُنْذُ ...) سافَرْتُ إلى ... (Last year/... ago) I travelled to ...

ولَكِنّي ما زُرْتُ ... But I didn't visit ...

____

____

____

____

43

Activity 3

Alex is talking about his study trip to the Middle East. Look at the cities and the sites they visited below. Think about which place fits in each gap in what Alex says. Then listen and write in the answers, as in the example.

الأَهْرام The Pyramids	عَمّان Amman	أَسْوان Aswan
الأُقْصُر Luxor	القاهِرة Cairo	طيبة Thebes
The Valley of the Kings وادي المُلوك	البَتْراء Petra	The West Bank [of Nile] البَرّ الغَرْبيّ
	وادي رُم Wadi Rum	

نَحنُ طَلَبة أمريكيّون. نَدرُس التاريخ
ونُحِبّ قِراءة الكُتُب القديمة.
في الشَّهر الماضي، سافَرْنا إلى ___القاهرة___
في مصر، ونَزَلْنا في فُندُق كبير أمام
________. بَعدَ ذلك، زُرْنا ________
في الجَنوب، ثُمَّ أَخَذْنا المَركَب إلى الشَّمال لنَذهَب إلى ________.
في البَرّ ________ من النَّهر، جَلَسْنا بجانِب مَعْبَد فِرعونيّ، وتَكَلَّمَ
الأساتِذة عَن وادي ________، وعَن ________ وهي العاصِمة القديمة.
بَعدَ ذلك أَخَذْنا الطائرة وسافَرْنا إلى الأُردُنّ. هناك، زُرْنا مدينة ________،
و________ رُم و________. نحن تَعَلَّمْنا الكثير في هذه الرِّحْلة،
وسَنَرجِع إلى ________ الأَوْسط في السنة القادمة وسَنَزور بِلاداً أُخرى!

Activity 4

Now read your completed transcript of what Alex says and decide if the following sentences are true (T) or false (F).

1 We visited Luxor, then we visited Aswan. ☐
2 We flew to the city of Amman in Jordan. ☐
3 We are Arab students who visited America. ☐
4 Our lecturers spoke to us about the Valley of the Queens. ☐
5 We are studying history. ☐
6 Last year, we visited Egypt. ☐
7 Next year, we will return to visit more countries. ☐

Part 2: Extension vocabulary

44

Arabic	Pronunciation	English	Write it yourself
ليبْيا/ليبيّ	*libyā/lībīy*	Libya/libyan	____________
السودان/سودانيّ	*as-sūdān/sūdānīy*	Sudan/Sudanese	____________
عُمان/عُمانيّ	*ʿumān/ʿumānīy*	Oman/Omani	____________
اليَمَن/يَمَنيّ	*al-yaman/yamanīy*	Yemen/Yemeni	____________
تونِس/تونِسيّ	*tūnis/tūnisīy*	Tunisia/Tunisian	____________
الجَزائِر/جَزائِريّ	*al-jazāʾir/jazāʾirīy*	Algeria/Algerian	____________
المَغْرِب/مَغْرِبيّ	*al-maghrib/ maghribīy*	Morocco/ Moroccan	____________
رِحْلة (ات)	*riḥla (āt)*	journey	____________
السِّياحة	*as-siyāḥa*	tourism	____________
مُسافِر (ون)	*musāfir (ūn)*	tourist/traveller	____________
الحَجّ	*al-ḥajj*	the pilgrimage	____________
جِنْسيّة (ات)	*jinsīyya (āt)*	nationality	____________
سِفارة (ات)	*sifāra (āt)*	embassy	____________
تأْشيرة (ات)	*taʾshīra (āt)*	visa	____________
غادَرَ/يُغادِر	*ghādara/yughādir*	to leave	____________
وَصَلَ/يَصِل	*waṣala/yaṣil*	to arrive	____________
أَدّى/يُؤَدّي	*adda/yuʾaddī*	to undertake	____________

Language tip

Wherever you travel in the Middle East, you will hear local dialects specific to the region. You may not fully understand the Arabic spoken on the street, and in the course of your studies you will probably want to gain a more detailed knowledge of at least one dialect. However, Modern Standard Arabic is a universal key that can act as a gateway to these dialects, and also to Arab culture and history in general.

Activity 5

You have seen these Arabic jobs advertised online. Look at the ads and then find the Arabic words and phrases to match the English below, as in the example.

Additional vocabulary

region مِنْطَقة   administration إدارة   departure(s) مُغادَرة

مَطلوب لِلعَمَل

تُعلِن الشركة العربيّة للسَفَر والسِّياحة عن الوَظائف التالية:

مَندوبون للمَبيعات	للعَمَل في مَكاتبنا في البِلاد الآتية: العراق، اليمن، السودان	احفظ
مُدير لمِنطَقة شَمال إفريقيا	الجِنسيّة: واحدة من بِلاد المغرب العربيّ: تونس، أو الجزائر، أو المغرب	احفظ
مُدير لرِحلات الحَجّ	إدارة التأشيرات مع السفارات السعوديّة إدارة الوُصول والمُغادرة في المطارات	احفظ
مُدير لمِنْطَقة أوروبا	مُدير لرِحلات السِّياحة في عَواصِم بِلاد غَرب أوروبا: باريس ولندن ومدريد وروما	احفظ

١ nationality
جنسيّة

٢ visas

٣ embassies

٤ manager

٥ employees

٦ arrival(s)

٧ Western Europe

٨ North Africa

٩ one of

١٠ capital cities

١١ wanted

١٢ Rome

Language tip

The 'Maghrib'

The Arabic word مَغرِب *maghrib* literally means 'place where the sun goes down' and is connected to the words for 'sunset', غُروب *ghurūb*, and 'west', غَرب *gharb*. The phrase المَغرِب العَرَبيّ *al-maghrib al-ɛarabīy*, 'The Arab Maghrib', refers to the whole of Arab north-west Africa. By itself, المَغرِب *al-maghrib* usually refers only to the country of Morocco.

Activity 6

Now look again at the Arabic jobs on page 48. Select the appropriate Arabic phrase for each of the statements below.

١ The company that needs new staff operates in the area of:

a المُستَشفيات **b** السَّفَر والسِّياحة **c** المدارس والجامعات

٢ The prefered nationality of the North Africa regional manager is:

a سوريّ أو لبنانيّ أو عراقيّ **b** مصريّ أو سودانيّ أو ليبيّ

c تونسيّ أو جزائريّ أو مغربيّ

٣ The company needs new sales reps in:

a ليبيا، الجزائر، مصر **b** لُندُن، مدريد، روما **c** العراق، اليمن، السودان

٤ The head of pilgrimage operations will work closely with:

a السِّفارات السعوديّة **b** الجامعات السعوديّة **c** السِّفارات الفَرَنسيّة

٥ The Western European capitals covered include:

a وارسو، أوسلو، دُبلِن **b** لُندُن، مدريد، روما **c** أثينا، برلين، ستوكهولم

Activity 7

45

Describe a recent journey. Use the prompts below to help you, and try to include as much of the vocabulary in this unit as you can. Play the model to review your pronunciation. Write down notes and then record yourself, or present to a group. You can also write up your description using your notes.

(السَّنة الماضية/مُنْذُ ...) زُرْتُ ... مع ... (Last year/... ago) I visited ... with ...

أَخَذْنا تأْشيرات مِن السِّفارة الـ... We took visas from the ... embassy

غادَرْنا ... وسافَرْنا بِالـ... إلى ... We left ... and travelled by ... to ...

نَزَلْنا في ... قَريب مِن ... We stayed in a ... near ...

ذَهَبْنا إلى ... في ... البَلَد. We went to ... in the ... of the country

كانَت الرِّحلة ... جِدّاً The journey was very ...

10 Shopping

Part 1: Core vocabulary

46

Arabic	Pronunciation	English	Write it yourself
التَّسَوُّق	*at-tasawwuq*	shopping	________
مَحَلّ (ات)	*maḥall (āt)*	shop, store	________
تاجِر (تُجّار)	*tājir/tujjār*	trader, merchant	________
سِعْر (أَسْعار)	*siɛr (asɛār)*	price	________
لَوْن (أَلْوان)	*lawn (alwān)*	colour	________
مَقاس (ات)	*maqās (āt)*	size	________
وَزْن (أَوْزان)	*wazn (awzān)*	weight	________
كيس (أَكْياس)	*kīs (akyās)*	bag, sack	________
مَصْنوع مِن	*maṣnūɛ min*	made of	________
ذَهَب	*dhahab*	gold	________
فِضّة	*fiḍḍa*	silver	________
نُحاس	*nuḥās*	copper	________
جِلْد	*jild*	leather	________
خَشَب	*khashab*	wood	________
قُطْن	*quṭn*	cotton	________
حَرير	*ḥarīr*	silk	________
بِكَمْ؟	*bi-kam?*	how much?	________
اِشْتَرى/يَشْتَري	*ishtara/yashtari*	to buy	________
باعَ/يَبيع	*bāɛa/yabīɛ*	to sell	________

47

Language tip

Words to describe colour

The basic Arabic colours follow a pattern, for example أبْيَض *abyaḍ* 'white', and أخْضَر *akhḍar* 'green', which become بَيْضاء *bayḍā'* and خَضْراء *khaḍrā'* for feminine or plural items. You can also expand your repertoire of colours into more subtle areas by adding an *-īy* ending to items of that colour. Listen to these examples:

لَيْمونيّ *laymūnīy* lemon-yellow ← لَيْمون *laymūn* lemons

زَيْتونيّ *zaytūnīy* olive-green ← زَيْتون *zaytūn* olives

رَماديّ *ramādīy* grey, ashen ← رَماد *ramād* ashes

Activity 1

Read what Maha says in English about her village market. Then match the Arabic phrases to the pictures, for example ١c.

"In our village square, Saturday is shopping day. There's an open market where you can buy almost anything! I bought my best ring there – 24-carat gold, they told me! My sister even bought a lemon-yellow silk kimono in this market. There's a trader from China who sells them in many colours and sizes. He also has cotton ones, but the price is less for cotton. My mother is planning on buying a grey bag there next Saturday, and my aunt will look for a wooden table."

١ كيمونو لَيْمونيّ من الحَرير

٢ أمّي وخالَتي

٣ حقيبة رَماديّة لأمّي

٤ خاتم ذَهَبيّ

٥ سِعره أغلى

٦ مائدة مَصْنوعة من الخَشَب

٧ يوم السَّبت القادِم

٨ تاجِر من الصين

d

c

b

a

h

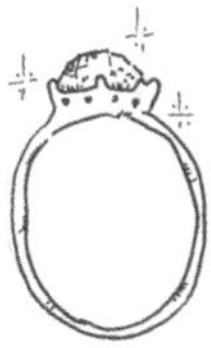

g

f

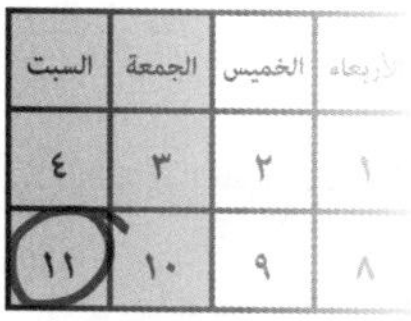

e

Activity 2

Now complete these Arabic sentences to match what you have learnt about Maha's village market, as in the example.

Additional vocabulary

village قَرْيَة   next القادِم   to look for بَحَثَ/يَبْحَث عَن

١ يوم السَّبت هو يوم ___السوق___ في قَرْيَتنا.

٢ اِشْتَرَتْ ___________ كيمونو ___________
مَصنوع من ___________.

٣ سَتَبْحَث خالَتي عن ___________ مَصنوعة من ___________.

٤ سَتَشْتَري أمّي ___________ رَماديّة يوم ___________ القادِم.

٥ تاجِر الكيمونو من ___________.
يَبيع الكيمونو بِـ___________ و___________ كثيرة.

٦ في السوق، ___________ خاتِمي المَصنوع ___________ الذَّهَب.

Activity 3

48

Imagine you want to go to the market in Maha's village to buy a particular item. Prepare some requests and questions using these prompts.

I'd like to buy ...	أُريد أن أَشْتَري ...
Is this made of ...?	هَل هذا (هذه) مَصْنوع(ة) مِن ...
How much is this one?	بِكَم هذا (هذه)؟
Do you have something bigger/cheaper?	هَلْ عِندَكُم شَيْء أكْبَر/أَرْخَص؟
Do you have other colours/sizes?	هَل عِندَكُم أَلْوان/مَقاسات أُخْرى؟

Practise out loud, listening to the model for help with pronunciation. When you are confident, write down your description.

____

____

____

____

Part 2: Extension vocabulary

49

Arabic	Pronunciation	English	Write it yourself
مَرْكَز التَّسَوُّق (مَراكِز التَّسَوُّق)	*markaz at-tasawwuq (marākiz at-tasawwuq)*	shopping centre, shopping mall	
بائِع (ون)	*bā'iع (ūn)*	seller	
تَخْفيض (ات)	*takhfīḍ (āt)*	discount	
عَرْض (عُروض)	*عarḍ (عurūḍ)*	offer	
تَوْصيل (ات)	*tawṣīl (āt)*	delivery	
حِساب (ات)	*ḥisāb (āt)*	account	
سَلّة (سِلال)	*salla (silāl)*	basket	
تاريخ الشِّراء	*tārīkh as-shirā'*	purchase date	
مَلابِس، أَزْياء	*malābis, azyā'*	clothes	
أَثاث	*athāth*	furniture	
صوف	*ṣūf*	wool	
بلاسْتيك	*blāstīk*	plastic	
وَرَق	*waraq*	paper	
طَلَبَ/يَطْلُب	*ṭalaba/yaṭlub*	to order	
بَحَثَ/يَبْحَث	*baḥatha/yabḥath*	to search	
جَرَّبَ/يُجَرِّب	*jarraba/yujarrib*	to try (on), to test	
فاصَلَ/يُفاصِل	*fāṣala/yufāṣil*	to barter, to haggle	

Cultural tip

Even if you can't go to a market or mall in the Arab World, there are still many interesting online shopping sites in the Middle East selling perfume, clothes, furniture and more. You can select the Arabic language option and wander around these websites at home.

Activity 4

Youssef is ordering from an online clothing retailer, *Spring Clothing*. First, look at the website and match the Arabic to the English.

١ عَرض خاصّ
٢ قُمْصان
٣ طَلَبي
٤ اِبْحَث
٥ سَلّة
٦ تَخْفيضات
٧ قُبّعات
٨ حِسابي

a my order
b basket
c hats
d search
e my account
f special offer
g discounts
h shirts

Activity 5

50

Youssef is now calling customer services at *Spring Clothing* and speaks to an agent called Samira. Listen to their conversation and read the transcript below. Then answer the questions about the conversation on page 55.

سميرة: أزياء الرَّبيع. صباح الخير. معك سميرة.

يوسف: صباح الخير. أنا اسمي يوسُف حِجازي. عندي حِساب معكم. اِشتَرَيْتُ قُبَّعة خضراء على الإنترنت.

سميرة: هل هناك مُشكِلة في المَقاس؟ في اللون؟

يوسف: لا. أنا لَم أُجرِّب القُبَّعة لأنّها لَم تَصِل بَعد.

سميرة: هل اِشتَرَيْتَ القُبَّعة في أُسبوع تخفيضات الرَّبيع؟

يوسف: لا أعرِف. كان هناك عَرض خاصّ على سِعر هذه القُبَّعات المَصنوعة من القُطن أو الصوف. أنا قُبَّعَتي خضراء وقُطنيّة.

سميرة: ما هو رَقم السَّلّة وتاريخ الشِّراء؟ سَأبحَث عَنها على الكمبيوتر.

يوسف: رَقم السَّلّة ٨٨ ت، وتاريخ الشِّراء الاثنين.

سميرة: الاثنين؟ ولكن اليوم الثُّلاثاء. هل اِشتَرَيْتَها أمس يا سَيِّد حِجازي؟

يوسف: نعم.

سميرة: تَناوَل إفطارك يا سَيِّد حِجازي. القُبَّعة في الطَّريق إلَيْك!

1 What day of the week does the conversation take place?

2 What has Youssef bought from the online retailer, *Spring Clothing*?

3 What is his problem with the order?

4 Does Youssef have an account with the retailer?

5 What basket number and sales date does he quote?

6 What suggestion does Samira have for Youssef, and why?

Activity 6

Now read the conversation again and choose the appropriate phrase to complete the sentence.

١ تَعمَل سميرة في ...
a مَصنَع أَحذِيَة b بيت حِجازي
c مَحَلّ أزياء الرَّبيع

٢ اِشتَرَى يوسف قُبَّعَته من ...
a الإنترنت b سَلّة سميرة
c سوق القَريَة

٣ قُبَّعة يوسف لَوْنها...
a أصفر b أزرق c أخضر

٤ قُبَّعة يوسف مَصنوعة من ...
a الصوف b القُطن c الجِلد

٥ القُبَّعة ...
a وَصَلَت أمس b سَتَصِل اليوم
c وَصَلَت اليوم

٦ تَرى سميرة أن يوسف عَلَيْه ...
a الاِنتِظار قَليلاً b أن يَأتي إلى
المَصنَع c أن يَختار لَوْناً مُختَلِفاً

٧ هاتَفَ يوسف سميرة صباح ...
a الاِثنين b الثُّلاثاء c الأربِعاء

٨ هناك عَرض خاصّ على سِعر ...
a الأزياء b القُبَّعات c الصوف

Activity 7

51 Talk about your shopping preferences and some items that you have bought recently. Use the prompts below and the vocabulary in this unit to get you started. Try to include opinions and reasons for your preferences. Play the model to review your pronunciation. You can also write up your talk using your notes. Present your work to an Arabic speaker if you can.

أُحِبّ أن أشتَري ... في السوق/مَركَز التَّسَوُّق. I like to buy ... in the market/the mall.

ولكنّي أُفَضِّل أن أشتَري ... على الإنترنت. But I prefer to buy ... on the Internet.

(لا) أُحِبّ أن أُفاصِل مَعَ البائِع. I (don't) like to bargain with the seller.

أمس/الأُسبوع الماضي، اِشتَرَيْتُ ... و... Yesterday/Last week, I bought ... and ...

هناك عُروض خاصّة/تَخفيضات على الأسعار.

There are special offers/discounts on the prices.

11 Food and drink

Part 1: Core vocabulary

52

Arabic	Pronunciation	English	Write it yourself
طَعام (أَطْعِمة)	*ṭaɛām (aṭɛima)*	food	
حِساب (ات)	*ḥisāb (āt)*	bill, check	
بَقّالة (ات)	*baqqāla (āt)*	grocery	
مَخْبَز (مَخابِز)	*makhbaz (makhābiz)*	bakery	
خَضْرَوات، خُضَريّ	*khaḍrawāt, khuḍarī*	vegetables, greengrocer	
لَحْم، لَحّام	*laḥm, laḥḥām*	meat, butcher	
سَمَك، سَمّاك	*samak, sammāk*	fish, fishmonger	
دَجاج	*dajāj*	chicken	
فَواكِه	*fawākih*	fruit	
خُبْز	*khubz*	bread	
حَليب	*ḥalīb*	milk	
شاي	*shāy*	tea	
قَهْوَة	*qahwa*	coffee	
ماء	*mā'*	water	
عَصير	*ɛaṣīr*	juice	
أَكَلَ/يَأْكُل	*akala/ya'kul*	to eat	
شَرِبَ/يَشْرَب	*shariba/yashrab*	to drink	
دَفَعَ/يَدْفَع	*dafaɛa/yadfaɛ*	to pay	
جَهَّزَ/يُجَهِّز	*jahhaza/yujahhiz*	to prepare	

Cultural tip

Be careful in the market!

The names of individual fruits and vegetables can vary from region to region in the Arab World. There is no 'standard' Arabic word for tomatoes, variously known as طماطم *ṭamāṭim*, بندورة *banadūra*, or قوطة *qūṭa*. Likewise, 'peaches' are known as خوخ *khawkh* or درّاق *durrāq*. The word خوخ *khawkh* can also refer to 'plums', which in other regions are known as برقوق *barqūq*.

Activity 1

What do I need? Choose the best answer according to what I want to do.

١ أريد أن أُجَهِّز سانْدَوِتش.

a عصير **b** خبز **c** شاي

٢ أريد أن أشتري خبزاً.

a حليب **b** دجاج **c** مخبز

٣ أريد أن أُجَهِّز الطعام.

a مطبخ **b** حساب **c** شاي

٤ أريد أن أُجَهِّز السَّلَطة.

a قهوة **b** حليب **c** خضروات

٥ أريد أن أدفَع.

a مطابخ **b** حساب **c** حليب

٦ أريد أن أشرَب عصيراً.

a فواكه **b** لحم **c** سمك

٧ أريد أن أغسل وجهي.

a قهوة **b** بقّالة **c** ماء

٨ أريد أن أشتري دجاجة.

a مخبز **b** لحّام **c** خضريّ

Activity 2

Match the words with the pictures, for example **١d**. Can you pronounce the words without their vowels?

١ الفواكه

٢ الدجاجة

٣ الشاي

٤ الحساب

٥ السمك

٦ الخبز

٧ قَهوَتي

٨ الخضروات

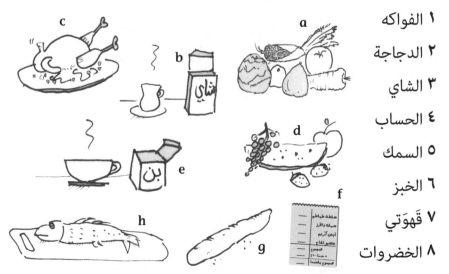

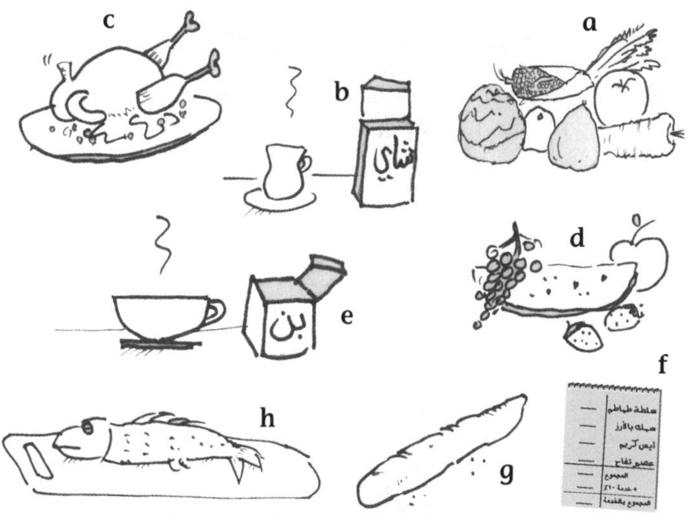

Activity 3

Now choose one of the words in Activity 2 on page 57 and write it in the gap, as in the example.

١ اِشتَرَيتُ هذا ___الخبز___ من المخبز.

٢ هذه __________. سَأَشْرَبُها الآن.

٣ هَل اِشتَرَيتَ هذه __________ من الخُضَريّ؟

٤ شَرِبنا عصير __________ في هذا المحلّ.

٥ اِشْتَرَيتُ هذا __________ من السمّاك.

٦ دَفَعوا __________ لصاحِبة المحلّ.

٧ اِشْتَرَتْ أمّي هذا __________ من البقّالة.

٨ اِشْتَرى أبي هذه __________ من اللحّام.

Activity 4

53

Imagine you want to go to town to buy some food and have a snack in a café. Prepare some requests and questions using these prompts.

أُريد أن أَشْتَري ... من الـ...	I'd like to buy ... from the ...
نُريد أن نَشرَب/أن نَأكُل ...	We'd like to drink/to eat ...
هَل عِندَكُم ...؟	Do you have ...?
مُمكِن (نِصف) كيلو ...؟	Can I have (half) a kilo of ...?
كَم الحِساب؟	How much is the bill?

Practise out loud, listening to the model for help with pronunciation. When you are confident, write down what you said.

____

____

____

____

____

Part 2: Extension vocabulary

54

Arabic	Pronunciation	English	Write it yourself
إفْطار	*ifṭār*	breakfast	_____
غَداء	*ghadā'*	lunch	_____
عَشاء	*ɛashā'*	dinner	_____
فُرْن (أَفْران)	*furn (afrān)*	oven	_____
طَبَق (أَطْباق)	*ṭabaq (aṭbāq)*	dish, plate	_____
كوب (أَكْواب)	*kūb (akwāb)*	glass	_____
سِكّين (سَكاكين)	*sikkīn (sakākīn)*	knife	_____
شَوْكة (شُوَك)	*shawka (shuwak)*	fork	_____
مِلْعَقة (مَلاعِق)	*milɛaqa (malāɛiq)*	spoon	_____
سَلَطة (ات)	*salaṭa (āt)*	salad	_____
مَشْوِيّ	*mashwī*	grilled	_____
مَقْلِيّ	*maqlī*	fried	_____
مَحْشِيّ	*maḥshī*	stuffed	_____
مَفْروم	*mafrūm*	minced	_____
مَسْلوق	*maslūq*	boiled	_____
مُقَطَّع	*muqaṭṭaɛ*	chopped	_____
تَناوَلَ/يَتَناوَل	*tanāwala/ yatanāwal*	to eat, to partake	_____

🔍 Cultural tip

Some dishes and drinks are common to the entire Middle East. For example, varieties of the following can be found throughout the region: ورق عنب *waraq ɛinab* 'stuffed vine leaves' (literally 'grape leaves'), فلافل *falāfil* 'falafel', باذنجان مخلّل *bādhinjān mukhallil* 'pickled aubergine', حمّص *ḥummuṣ* 'chick peas', طحينة *ṭaḥīna* 'tahini', سلطة الزبادي *salaṭat az-zabādī* 'yoghurt salad', and شاي بالنعناع *shāy bin-naɛnāɛ* 'tea with mint'.

Activity 5

Zaid and Dina's engagement party is next Thursday. Dina's mother has made a list of dishes for all the family to prepare.

Additional vocabulary

soup حَساء   prawns جَمبَريّ   vinegar خَلّ   celery كَرَفْس

أطباق لحَفل خُطوبة زيد ودينا

- ثلاث دجاجات مسلوقة للحَساء، مع الفِلفِل الأسود
- ثلاث دجاجات مطبوخة في الفرن مع البطاطس والثوم
- ثلاث سمكات مشوية، وثلاث مقلية، مع الأرزّ بالبَصَل الأحمر
- ورق عنب وباذنجان محشي باللحم المفروم
- خمس سلطات في خمسة أطباق:
  - الطماطم المقطّعة مع الجُبن والزيت
  - الحمّص مع الزّيتون والخيار
  - الجَمبَريّ مع الخَلّ والليمون
  - الجزَر مع الكَرَفس والزّبيب
  - الزبادي مع النّعناع والثوم

Dina's mother is looking through the list of dishes and deciding what they need to buy from each shop. Complete her table below with the items needed, as in the examples.

البقّالة	الخضريّ	السمّاك	اللحّام
فِلفِل أسود *(black pepper)*			٦ دجاجات *(6 chickens)*

55

Activity 6

Hassan lives a busy life. Listen to what he says about his eating habits and see if you can hear and read the Arabic phrases below in what he says, as in the example.

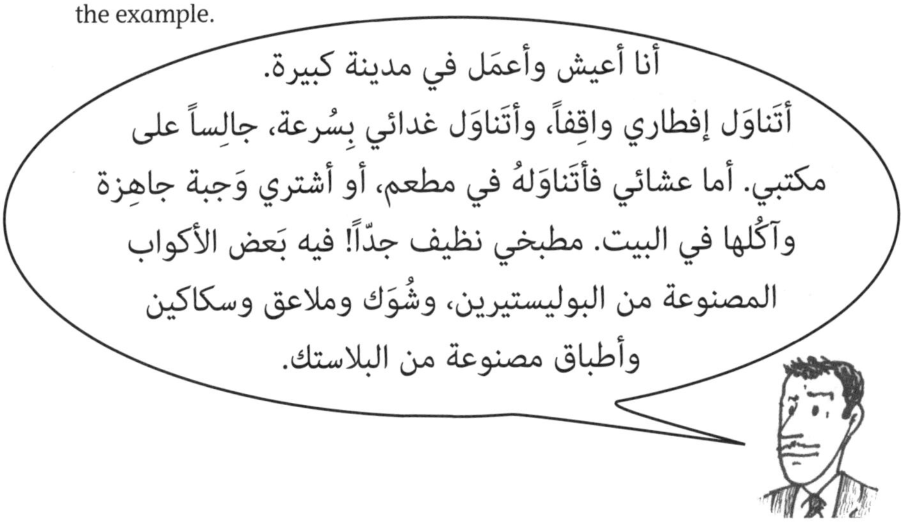
أنا أعيش وأعمَل في مدينة كبيرة.
أتَناوَل إفطاري واقِفاً، وأتَناوَل غدائي بِسُرعة، جالِساً على مكتبي. أما عشائي فأتَناوَلهُ في مطعم، أو أشتري وَجبة جاهِزة وآكُلها في البيت. مطبخي نظيف جدّاً! فيه بَعض الأكواب المصنوعة من البوليستيرين، وشُوَك وملاعق وسكاكين وأطباق مصنوعة من البلاستك.

١ I eat my breakfast

أتناول إفطاري

٢ standing up

______

٣ sitting down at my desk

______

٤ as for my dinner

______

٥ a ready meal

______

٦ I eat it in the house

______

٧ made from polystyrene

______

٨ made from plastic

______

56

Activity 7

Talk about your eating habits. Use the prompts below and Activity 6 to help you. Play the model to review your pronunciation. You can also write up your talk using your notes. Present your work to an Arabic speaker if you can.

أنا أعيش وأعمَل في ... I live and work in ...

أَشتَري طَعامي مِن ... I buy my food from ...

أَتَناوَل إفطاري/غَدائي/عَشائي ... I eat my breakfast/lunch/dinner ...

كُلّ يَوم، أُجَهِّز عَشائي في ... Every day, I prepare my dinner in ...

وَجبَتي المُفَضَّلة هي ... My favourite meal is ...

أنا (لا) آكُل وَجَبات جاهِزة كَثيراً I (don't) eat ready meals much

12 Going out

Part 1: Core vocabulary

57

Arabic	Pronunciation	English	Write it yourself
أَوَّلاً	*awwalan*	firstly	____________
أَخيراً	*akhīran*	finally	____________
ثُمَّ	*thumma*	then	____________
قَبْلَ/بَعْدَ ذَلِك	*qabla/ baɛda dhālika*	before/after that	____________
الطَّقْس	*aṭ-ṭaqs*	the weather	____________
مُشْمِس	*mushmis*	sunny	____________
مُمْطِر	*mumṭir*	rainy	____________
غائِم	*ghā'im*	cloudy	____________
مَتْحَف (مَتاحِف)	*matḥaf (matāḥif)*	museum	____________
حَديقة (حَدائِق)	*ḥadīqa (ḥadā'iq)*	park	____________
سينِما (سينِمات)	*sīnima (sīnimāt)*	cinema	____________
مَسْرَح (مَسارِح)	*masraḥ (masāriḥ)*	theatre	____________
صَديق (أَصْدِقاء)	*ṣadiq (aṣdiqā')*	friend	____________
شاهَدَ/يُشاهِد	*shāhada/yushāhid*	to watch, to view	____________
قابَلَ/يُقابِل	*qābala/yuqābil*	to meet	____________
حَجَزَ/يَحْجِز	*ḥajaza/yaḥjiz*	to reserve	____________
ضَحِكَ/يَضْحَك	*ḍaḥika/yaḍḥak*	to laugh	____________
اِسْتَمْتَعَ/ يَسْتَمْتِع بِ	*istamtaɛa/ yastamtiɛ bi-*	to enjoy	____________

Activity 1

Choose the best drawing to complete the sentences.

١ الطقس مُمطِر اليوم.
أنا سَآخُذ ...

a  b  c 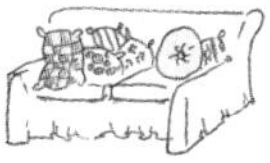

٢ الطقس مُشمِس اليوم.
سَنَذهَب إلى ...

a  b  c 

٣ الطقس غائم اليوم.
أنا لَنْ آخُذ ...

a  b  c 

٤ الطقس مُمطِر اليوم.
سَنَذهَب إلى ...

a  b  c 

٥ حَجَزْتُ لِأُشاهِد مَسرَحيّة.
سَأذهَب إلى ...

a  b  c 

٦ سَيَأكُل أصدِقائي عِندي.
سَأذهَب إلى ...

a  b  c 

٧ سَنَرى لوحات «بيكاسو».
سَنَذهَب إلى ...

a  b 

c 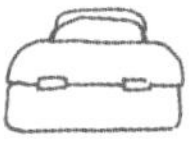

Activity 2

58

Use the prompts below to invite a friend to go out with you. You can include more than one activity using the connecting words and phrases in the list opposite. Listen to the model for help with pronunciation and don't forget to try and record yourself. When you are confident, write down what you said.

The weather is ... today.	الطَّقْس ... اليَوْم.
Would you like to go to the ...?	هَل تُريد(ين) أن تَذْهَب(ي) إلى الـ...؟
I have reserved to see ... at the ...	حَجَزْتُ لِأُشاهِد ... في الـ...

____

____

____

____

Activity 3

59

Shukri and his wife, Zahra, are being interviewed for a documentary about how couples met. Listen to the interview, reading the Arabic transcript. Then complete the English translation below, as in the example.

شُكريّ: أنا مِصريّ، وأعمَل في مَتحَف كبير، واسمي شُكريّ.

زَهرة: وأنا زَهرة. أنا مُمَثِّلة في المَسرَح.

شُكريّ: في صباح مُمطِر، قابَلْتُ زَهرة على سُلَّم المَسرَح

زَهرة: كُنْتُ أمشي بِسُرعة نَحوَ الباب وهو كانَ مع كَلبه، تيتو.

شُكريّ: قُلْتُ لَها: "لِماذا تَمشين بِسُرعة، والطقس مُمطِر، والماء في كلّ مَكان؟!"

زَهرة: قُلْتُ لَهُ: "أوَّلاً، نَتعارَف! ما اسم ... هذا الكلب الجميل؟"

شُكريّ: ضَحِكْنا، وبَعدَ ذلك أصْبَحْنا أصدِقاء، أنا وهي وتيتو!

زَهرة: اِستَمتَعْنا مَعاً بالمَشي في الحَدائق، ومُشاهَدة الأفلام في السينما.

شُكريّ: وأخيراً، تَزَوَّجْنا مُنذُ عِشرين سَنة!

Shukri: I'm *Egyptian*. I work in a large __________. My name is Shukri.

Zahra: And I'm Zahra. I'm an actress in the __________.

Shukri: One __________ morning. I __________ Zahra on the steps of the __________.

Zahra: I was __________ quickly towards the __________ and he was with his __________, Tito.

Shukri: I __________ to her: "Why are you walking quickly when the __________ is rainy and the __________ is everywhere?!".

Zahra: I __________ to him: "__________, let's get aquainted! What's the name of … this __________ dog?".

Shukri: We __________, and __________ that we became __________, me and her and Tito!

Zahra: We both __________ walking in the __________ and watching films in the __________.

Shukri: And __________, we got married __________ years ago.

Part 2: Extension vocabulary

60

Arabic	Pronunciation	English	Write it yourself
ريف (أرْياف)	*rīf (aryāf)*	countryside	___________
صَحْراء (صَحارى)	*ṣaḥrā' (ṣaḥāra)*	desert	___________
مِنْطَقة (مَناطِق)	*minṭaqa (manāṭiq)*	region, area	___________
جَبَل (جِبال)	*jabal (jibāl)*	mountain	___________
قَلْعة (قِلاع)	*qalɛa (qilāɛ)*	fort, castle	___________
واحة (ات)	*wāḥa (āt)*	oasis	___________
نَخْلة (نَخيل)	*nakhla (nakhīl)*	palm tree	___________
شاطئ (شَواطِئ)	*shāṭi' (shawāṭi')*	beach	___________
بَحْر (بِحار)	*baḥr (biḥār)*	sea	___________
طَبيعيّ	*ṭabīɛīy*	natural	___________
صَحْراويّ	*ṣaḥrāwīy*	desert-like	___________
ريفيّ	*rīfīy*	rustic, rural	___________
رَأى/يَرى	*ra'a/yara*	to see	___________
شَمَّ/يَشُمّ	*shamma/yashumm*	to smell	___________
قادَ/يَقود (سَيّارة)	*qāda/yaqūd (sayyāra)*	to drive (a car)	___________
سَبَحَ/يَسْبَح	*sabaḥa/yasbaḥ*	to swim	___________
تَوَجَّهَ/ يَتَوَجَّه (نَحْوَ)	*tawajjaha/ yatawajjah (naḥwa)*	to head (towards)	___________

Language tip

Names of places in the Middle East can have specific meanings in Arabic. For example, the Arabic for Bahrain, البحرين *al-baḥrayn*, literally means 'the two seas'. Likewise the Sahara Desert comes from the Arabic word for 'deserts', صحارى *ṣaḥāra*. Sometimes these familiar connections can help you to retain vocabulary.

Language tip

Verbal nouns

Nouns are formed from verbs in English by adding endings such as *-ing*, *-tion*, or *-ment*. In Arabic, verbal nouns also follow patterns but these are changes within the word based on the root letters rather than endings. The verbal noun patterns vary for basic verbs. For example, ذَهاب *dhahāb* 'going' from the verb ذَهَبَ/يَذهب *dhahāba/yadh-hab* 'to go'; or جُلوس *julūs* 'sitting' from the verb جَلَسَ/يَجلِس *jalasa/yajlis* 'to sit'. However, the verbal noun patterns are largely predictable for the forms (or variations) of the verb. For example, تَجْهيز *tajhīz* 'preparation' from the verb جَهَّزَ/يُجَهِّز *jahhaza/yujahhiz* 'to prepare', or إدارة *idāra* 'management/administration' from the verb أدارَ/يُدير *adāra/yudīr* 'to manage/to administer'. A good dictionary will show the verbal nouns alongside the verbs.

It is common in Arabic to use a verbal noun following an initial verb, so it is useful to understand how they work. Look at the following ways of expressing the same meaning, using two verbs or a verbal noun:

أُحِبّ أن أَذهَب إلى السينما. / أُحِبّ الذَّهاب إلى السينما.

(I like to go to the cinema.)

نُفَضِّل أن نَجلِس في المَقْهى. / نُفَضِّل الجُلوس في المَقْهى.

(We prefer to sit in the café.)

Activity 4

Match the verbs with the relevant nouns, for example **١f**.
Then write the English meanings next to the Arabic.

١ سَبَحَ/يَسْبَح *to swim*		a قِيادة ______
٢ قابَلَ/يُقابِل ______		b حَجْز ______
٣ تَوَجَّهَ/يَتَوَجَّه ______		c مُشاهَدة ______
٤ قادَ/يَقود ______		d زِيارة ______
٥ اِسْتَمْتَعَ/يَسْتَمْتِع ______		e شَمّ ______
٦ شاهَدَ/يُشاهِد ______		f سِباحة *swimming*
٧ شَمَّ/يَشُمّ ______		g ضَحِك ______
٨ حَجَزَ/يَحْجِز ______		h اِسْتِمْتاع ______
٩ زارَ/يَزور ______		i مُقابَلة ______
١٠ ضَحِكَ/يَضْحَك ______		j تَوَجُّه ______

Activity 5

Amir is Tunisian. He is telling a friend in an email about what he likes to do in his time off. Look at the email and then answer the questions below. Don't worry about understanding every word. Concentrate on getting the gist.

Additional vocabulary

pleasant لَطيف   holidays عُطلات   summer الصَّيْف   winter الشِّتاء

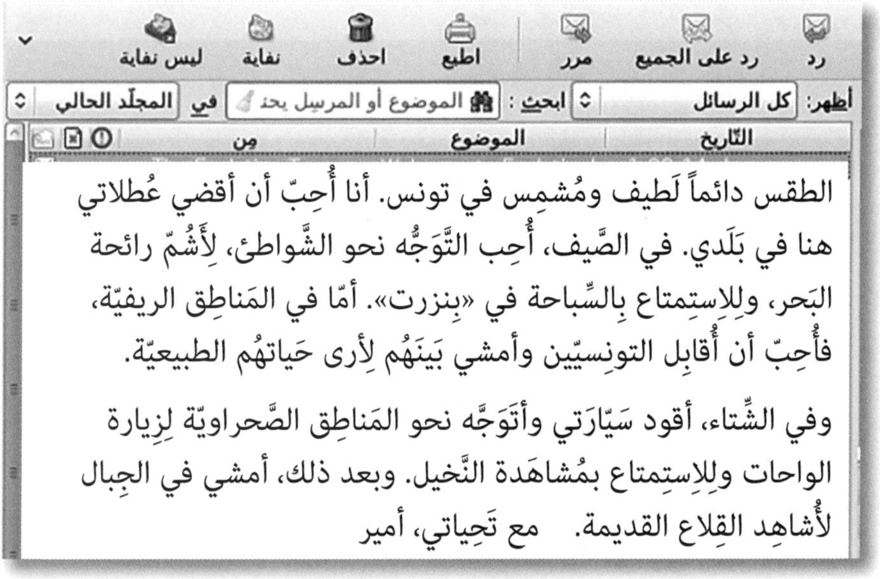

1 How does Amir describe the weather in Tunisia?

2 Does Amir like to go abroad for his holidays?

3 Why does he like to go to the beaches in summer?

4 What does he like to do in the rural areas?

5 Why does he head for desert regions in winter?

6 What does Amir look at while walking in the mountains?

Activity 6

61

Talk about how you like to spend your time off. Use the prompts below and Amir's email to help you. Write down notes first, and then record yourself. Play the model to review your pronunciation. You can also write up your description using your notes. Show your work to an Arabic speaker if you can.

In ..., the weather is always ... and ... في ... ، الطَّقس دائماً ... و...

I like to spend my holidays ... أنا أُحِبّ أن أقضي عُطلاتي ...

In the summer/the winter, I head for ... في الصَّيف/الشِّتاء، أتَوَجَّه نَحوَ ...

I enjoy visiting ... أسْتَمْتِع بِزِيارة ...

I walk/I drive in the ... to look at ... أمشي/أقود سَيّارَتي في الـ... لأُشاهِد ...

13 Everyday life

Part 1: Core vocabulary

62

Arabic	Pronunciation	English	Write it yourself
كُلّ يَوْم	*kull yawm*	every day	________
دائِماً	*dā'iman*	always	________
عادةً	*عādatan*	usually	________
أَحْياناً	*aḥyānan*	sometimes	________
أَيّام الـ...	*ayyām al...*	on ... days	________
الساعة ...	*as-sāعa ...*	at ... o'clock	________
الساعة...والنِّصْف	*as-sāعa ... wan-niṣf*	at half past ...	________
الساعة ... والرُّبْع	*as-sāعa ... war-rubع*	at quarter past ...	________
الساعة ... والثُّلْث	*as-sāعa ... wath-thulth*	at twenty ('a third') past ...	________
دَقيقة (دَقائِق)	*daqīqa (daqā'iq)*	minute	________
مَتى؟	*mata?*	when?	________
حالة (ات)	*ḥāla (āt)*	state, condition	________
صَحا/يَصْحو	*ṣaḥa/yaṣḥū*	to wake up	________
نامَ/يَنام	*nāma/yanām*	to sleep	________
لَبِسَ/يَلْبَس	*labisa/yalbas*	to wear, to put on	________
غَسَلَ/يَغْسِل	*ghasala/yaghsil*	to wash	________
لَعِبَ/يَلْعَب	*laعiba/yalعab*	to play	________
خَرَجَ/يَخْرُج	*kharaja/yakhruj*	to leave, to go out	________

63

Language tip

Telling the time
When you're telling the time in standard Arabic, you need to use the 'ordinal' numbers (first, second, third, etc.), rather than the 'cardinal' numbers (one, two, three, etc.). Listen to these examples:

الساعة الخامسة *as-sāɛa al-khāmisa* five o'clock (literally 'the fifth hour')

الساعة الثالِثة والنِّصف *as-sāɛa al-thālitha wan-niṣf* half-past three (literally 'the third hour and the half')

الساعة العاشِرة والثُّلث *as-sāɛa al-ɛāshira wath-thulth* twenty past ten (literally 'the tenth hour and the third')

الساعة الواحِدة وسِتّ دَقائق *as-sāɛa al-wāḥida wa sitt daqā'iq* six minutes past one (literally 'the first hour and six minutes')

Activity 1

Choose the clock which shows the correct time, for example **١b**.

١ الساعة الرابِعة
a  **b**  **c** 

٢ الساعة الثامِنة
a  **b**  **c** 

٣ الساعة الثانية والنِّصف
a  **b**  **c** 

٤ الساعة الخامِسة والنِّصف
a  **b**  **c** 

٥ الساعة التاسِعة والرُّبع
a  **b**  **c** 

٦ الساعة السادِسة والرُّبع
a  **b**  **c** 

٧ الساعة التاسِعة والثُّلث
a  **b**  **c** 

٨ الساعة العاشِرة وخَمس دَقائق
a  **b**  **c** 

٩ الساعة الرابِعة وعَشر دَقائق
a  **b**  **c** 

Activity 2

Write the missing Arabic words in the sentences to match the English translation, as in the example.

Every day, I wake up at half past seven.	١ كلّ يوم، ___أَصْحو___ الساعة ______ والنصف.
After that I wash my face.	٢ بَعدَ ذلك ______ وَجهي.
I look out of the window to see what the weather is like.	٣ أنظُر من ______ لِأرى حالة ______.
I usually have breakfast at eight o'clock.	٤ ______ أتَناوَل إفطاري الساعة ______.
Sometimes I do ('I play') some light exercise.	٥ أحياناً ______ بَعضَ الرياضة ______.
I leave the house at quarter past nine.	٦ ______ من البيت الساعة التاسعة و______.

Activity 3

64

Talk about your morning routine. Use the prompts below to say what you do in the mornings. You can vary the order or how ofen you do certain things.

كلّ يوم أصْحو الساعة ...	Every day I wake up at ...
أنا دائماً ...	I always ...
أنا أحياناً ...	I sometimes ...
أتَناوَل إفطاري الساعة ...	I eat my breakfast at ...
عادةً أخْرُج من البَيت الساعة ...	I usually leave the house at ...

Practise out loud, listening to the model for help with pronunciation. When you are confident, write down what you said.

____

____

____

____

____

Part 2: Extension vocabulary

65

Arabic	Pronunciation	English	Write it yourself
عادة (ات)	*ɛāda (āt)*	routine, habit	________
نادِراً	*nādiran*	rarely	________
لا ... أبَداً	*lā ... abadan*	never	________
طَوالَ ...	*ṭawāla ...*	all ... long	________
حَوالَيْ	*ḥawālay*	about, approximately	________
وَجْه (وُجوه)	*wajh (wajūh)*	face	________
سِنّ (أسْنان)	*sinn (asnān)*	tooth	________
ذَقْن (ذُقون)	*dhaqn (dhuqūn)*	chin	________
شَعْر	*shaɛr*	hair	________
اِسْتَيْقَظَ/يَسْتَيْقِظ	*istayqaẓa/yastayqiẓ*	to get up	________
نَظَّفَ/يُنَظِّف	*naẓẓafa/yunaẓẓif*	to clean	________
رَتَّبَ/يُرَتِّب	*rattaba/yurattib*	to tidy	________
أَعَدَّ/يُعِدّ	*aɛadda/yuɛidd*	to prepare, to get ready	________
حَلَقَ/يَحْلِق	*ḥalaqa/yaḥliq*	to shave	________
وَقَفَ/يَقِف	*waqafa/yaqif*	to stand	________
فَكَّرَ/يُفَكِّر	*fakkara/yufakkir*	to think	________
نَسِيَ/يَنْسى	*nasiya/yansa*	to forget	________

! Language tip

In Arabic, you cannot simply 'shave'. You need to add the area that you are shaving, most commonly the 'chin'. So the phrase 'I shave before breakfast' would become 'I shave my chin before breakfast':

أحلِق ذَقني قَبلَ الإفطار *aḥliq daqnī qabla l-ifṭār.*

Activity 4

Nur has produced a commentary about her morning routine for her fitness instructor. Read the first part of her commentary and pick out the Arabic equivalents of the phrases below, as in the example.

Additional vocabulary

diary يَوْمِيّات　part جُزْء　kettle غَلّاية ماء　according to حَسَبَ

يَوْمِيّات نور: الجُزء الأوَّل

الساعة السادسة إلى الساعة السادسة و٣٠ دقيقة، أو ٣٢ دقيقة – حَسَبَ البَيضة المَسلوقة

كلّ يوم، أصحو الساعة السادسة وأتَوَجَّه نحوَ غلّاية الماء في المطبخ. بعد ذلك أتَوَجَّه نحوَ الحمّام لِأغسِل وَجهي، وأنظُر من شبّاك الحمّام لِأرى حالة الطَّقس في هذا الصباح. ثمّ أرجِع إلى المطبخ لِأُجَهِّز كوب الشاي الأوَّل. أقِف في وَسَط المطبخ وأُفَكِّر في إفطاري، وفي حالة الطَّقس، وملابسي لِليوم. بعد ذلك، أخرُج من المطبخ وأتَوَجَّه نحوَ غُرفة الطعام ومعي الشاي وأي طعام يُقابِلني بين وَسَط المطبخ والمائدة. عادةً أَتَناوَل إفطاري في حَوالَيْ خمس دقائق وأحياناً في سبع، إذا كانَ في طَبَقي بَيضة مَسلوقة.

١ I head towards

أتوجّه نحو

٢ the bathroom window

____

٣ what the weather is like

____

٤ the first glass of tea

____

٥ I think about my breakfast

____

٦ any food that encounters me

____

٧ if there is

____

٨ a boiled egg

____

Activity 5

Nur's commentary continues. Read the second part and decide if the sentences below are true (T) or false (F).

يَوْمِيّات نور: الجُزء الثاني

الساعة السادسة و٣٠ دقيقة ، أو ٣٢ دقيقة
إلى الساعة السابعة والربع

أنا لا أشرَب القهوة أبَداً. ولِذلك، أرجِع إلى غُرفة نومي بَعدَ الإفطار لِأُرَتِّبها قليلاً، ولِأُعِدّ ما سَألبَسه اليوم فَوقَ سريري. نادِراً، ألعَب بَعضَ الرياضة الخفيفة، ولكنّي عادةً أنسى. بعد ذلك، أرجِع إلى الحمّام لِأُنَظِّف أسناني، ولِأغسِل شَعري. وقَبلَ أن أخرُج من الحمّام، أنظُر من الشبّاك لِأرى حالة الطقس مَرّة أُخرى. وأخيراً، أشكُر اللّه لأنّي سَيِّدة ولا أحتاج إلى أن أحلِق ذَقني كلّ صباح مِثل أبي وأخي! أخرُج من البيت الساعة السابعة والربع.

1 Nur's morning routine lasts an hour and a quarter in total. ☐

2 She always drinks coffee in the morning. ☐

3 She lays the clothes she will wear on her bed in the morning. ☐

4 Nur often works out in the morning. ☐

5 She sometimes forgets to clean her teeth. ☐

6 She looks at the weather from the window twice during the morning. ☐

7 Unlike her father and brother, Nur doesn't need to shave every morning. ☐

8 She leaves the house at half past seven. ☐

Activity 6

Write a commentary about your own evening routine. Use Nur's commentary and the words and phrases in this unit to help you. You could deliver the commentary as a presentation. Include videos/photos if you can. Show your work to a native speaker or post it in an online forum if you're feeling brave.

14 Society and current affairs

Part 1: Core vocabulary

66

Arabic	Pronunciation	English	Write it yourself
مُجْتَمَع (ات)	*mujtamaɛ (āt)*	society	________
حُكومة (ات)	*ḥukūma (āt)*	government	________
صِناعة (ات)	*ṣināɛa (āt)*	industry	________
دين (أَدْيان)	*dīn (adyān)*	religion	________
حَياة (حَيَوات)	*ḥayāh (ḥayawāt)*	life	________
مُسْتَقْبَل	*mustaqbal*	future	________
صِحّة	*ṣiḥḥa*	health	________
سَعادة	*saɛāda*	happiness	________
اِقْتِصاد	*iqtiṣād*	economy	________
مَلِك (مُلوك)	*malik (mulūk)*	king	________
أَمير (أُمَراء)	*amīr (umarā')*	emir, prince	________
وَزير (وُزَراء)	*wazīr (wuzarā')*	minister	________
رَئيس (رُؤَساء)	*ra'īs (ru'asā')*	president, head	________
شَعْب (شُعوب)	*shaɛb (shuɛūb)*	people, populace	________
عيد (أَعْياد)	*ɛīd (aɛyād)*	feast, festival	________
جَميع	*jamīɛ*	every, everyone	________
بَنى/يَبْني	*bana/yabnī*	to build	________
ساعَدَ/يُساعِد	*sāɛada/yusāɛid*	to help, to assist	________
اِسْتَقْبَلَ/يَسْتَقْبِل	*istaqbala/yastaqbil*	to receive (*guests, etc.*)	________

Activity 1

Match the singular words with their plurals, for example ١c. Then write the English meanings, as in the example.

١ مَلِك	*king*	a صِناعات	______
٢ حُكومة	______	b أديان	______
٣ وَزير	______	c مُلوك	*kings*
٤ عيد	______	d مُجتَمَعات	______
٥ شَعب	______	e وُزَراء	______
٦ صِناعة	______	f حُكومات	______
٧ دين	______	g شُعوب	______
٨ مُجتَمَع	______	h أعياد	______

> **! Language tip**
>
> **Uncountables**
>
> Some words such as صِحّة *ṣiḥḥa* 'health' and سَعادة *saɛāda* 'happiness' do not have a commonly used plural. As in English, they are 'uncountable'.
>
> صِحّة أُمّي *ṣiḥḥat ummī* the health of my mother
>
> صِحّة أُمَّهاتِنا *ṣiḥḥat ummahātinā* the health of our mothers
>
> سَعادة الشَّعب *saɛādat ash-shaɛb* the happiness of the people
>
> سَعادة كلّ شُعوب *saɛādat kull shuɛūb* the happiness of all peoples

Activity 2

67

Express your views and opinions about society. Use the prompts below to help you. Don't forget to listen to the model for help with pronunciation and record yourself. When you are confident, write down what you said.

أَعْتَقِد/في رَأْيي ... I think/In my opinion ...

أَهَمّ شَيْء في الحَياة هو ... The most important thing in life is ...

عَلَيْنا أن نَبْني/نُساعِد ... We should build/help ...

____

____

____

Activity 3

The Prime Minister's office has sent out the messages below on social media in the past few days. Each message reflects one of these general themes:

- public holiday
- general inspiration
- visiting dignitaries
- the economy

Choose a theme and write it next to the appropriate message below.

1 ______________

____

2 ______________

____

3 ______________

____

4 ______________

____

Activity 4

Now complete the translations of the messages, as in the example.

1 Special *thanks* to the Minister of the ______________ who has ______________ me. Our ______________ is strong and is growing every ______________!

2 Happy ______________ on the occasion of ______________ Day. ______________ and ______________ to all the ______________!

3 I ______________ a group of ______________ today. The ______________ is bright for ______________!

4 The ______________ is working for ______________ seven ______________ a week. Together we will ______________ a better ______________!

Part 2: Extension vocabulary

68

Arabic	Pronunciation	English	Write it yourself
اِنْتِخاب (ات)	*intikhāb (āt)*	election	___________
قانون (قَوانين)	*qānūn (qawānīn)*	law	___________
ثَقافة (ات)	*thaqāfa (āt)*	culture	___________
تَقْليد (تقاليد)	*taqlīd (taqālīd)*	tradition	___________
عَقْل (عُقول)	*ɛaql (ɛuqūl)*	mind, reason	___________
حَرْب (حُروب)	*ḥarb (ḥurūb)*	war	___________
سَلام	*salām*	peace	___________
مَناخ	*manākh*	climate	___________
مُؤَسَّسة خَيْريّة (مُؤَسَّسات خَيْريّة)	*mu'assasa khayrīyya (mu'assasāt khayrīyya)*	charity ('charitable institution')	___________
مُفيد	*mufīd*	beneficial	___________
ضارّ	*ḍārr*	harmful	___________
فَقير (فُقَراء)	*faqīr (fuqarā')*	poor (person)	___________
نَبيل (نُبَلاء)	*nabīl (nubalā')*	noble (person)	___________
مَريض (مَرْضى)	*marīḍ (marḍa)*	sick (person)	___________
مُسِنّ (ون)	*musinn (ūn)*	elderly (person)	___________
شَجَّعَ/يُشَجِّع	*shajjaɛa/yushajjiɛ*	to encourage	___________
تَطَوَّعَ/يَتَطَوَّع	*taṭawwaɛa/ yataṭawwaɛ*	to volunteer	___________
اِحْتَفَلَ/يَحْتَفِل بِـ	*iḥtafala/yaḥtafil bi-*	to celebrate	___________
تَبَرَّعَ/يَتَبَرَّع	*tabarraɛa/ yatabarraɛ*	to donate	___________

Language tip

Making nouns into adjectives

The -*īy* ending (*nisba*), employed to create different colours (see page 52), can be used generally to make adjectives from a wide variety of nouns. For example, أسبوعيّ *usbūʿīy* 'weekly' from أسبوع *usbūʿ* 'week'; or خيريّ *khayrīy* 'charitable' from خير *khayr* 'charity, good works'.

Remember to remove any *tā' marbūṭa* ending from the noun before adding the -*īy* ending. For example, حكوميّ *ḥukūmīy* 'governmental' from حكومة *ḥukūma* 'government'.

Activity 5

Using the vocabulary lists in this unit (pages 74 and 77) and the Language tip above, create Arabic adjectives that match the English below, as in the example.

١ legal ___قانونيّ___

٢ economic ____________

٣ cultural ____________

٤ religious ____________

٥ industrial ____________

٦ traditional ____________

٧ popular ____________

٨ healthy ____________

٩ mental, rational ____________

Activity 6

Farida is a speaker at a rally organised by 'The Community Party'. She is young and doesn't have children, but is very interested in volunteering and charity work. Look at Farida at the rally and then read the slogans at the top of page 79 that she sees around her on the rally banners and posters. Which three messages do you think would interest Farida most?

☆ التَّبَرُّع للمُؤَسَّسات الخيريّة من التَّقاليد الجميلة في بِلادنا

☆ الأُسرة تُشَجِّع الأطفال على تَعَلُّم كلّ ما هو مُفيد

☆ حينَ نَحتَفِل بالأعياد يَجِب أن نَتَذَكَّر الفَقير والمَريض والمُسِنّ

☆ السَّلام أفضَل من الحُروب في بِناء مُستَقبَل الشُّعوب

☆ العَمَل التَّطَوُّعيّ يَبني الشَّخصيّة النَّبيلة

☆ العِلم والثَّقافة غِذاء للعَقل السَّليم

Activity 7

Look again at the Arabic slogans above that Farida saw at the rally. Select the appropriate Arabic phrase to complete each of the statements below.

١ We should remember the poor, the sick and the old when:

a نَحتَفِل بالصِّحّة b نَحتَفِل بالأعياد c نُساعِد الحُكومة

٢ Peace is better than war in building:

a مُستَقبَل التَّطَوُّع b شَخصيّات الشُّعوب c مُستَقبَل الشُّعوب

٣ One of the great traditions of our country is:

a التَّبَرُّع للمُؤَسَّسات التَّقليديّة b التَّبَرُّع للمُؤَسَّسات العَقليّة

c التَّبَرُّع للمُؤَسَّسات الخَيريّة

٤ Everything beneficial children learn is encouraged by:

a الأُسرة b الاِنتِخابات c الحُكومة

٥ Knowledge and culture are food for:

a العَقل النَّبيل b العَقل السَّليم c الأُسرة السَّليمة

٦ The noble character is built by:

a العَمَل التَّطَوُّعيّ b العَقل التَّطَوُّعيّ c العَمَل الصِّناعيّ

Activity 8

Have a go at producing some of your own slogans and messages. Use the examples in this unit to help you. You could illustrate the slogans as posters or format your messages for social media. Include videos/photos if you can. Show your slogans and messages to a native speaker, send them to any Arabic-speaking friends, or post them online. It's a good way of communicating in Arabic to the wider world. You might even get some replies!

Answers to activities

Unit 1

Activity 1

١ أَنا أَحْمَد. ٢ أَنا سَحَر. ٣ نَحْنُ حَمْدي وَمُحَمَّد.
٤ هَلْ أَنْتِ سَحَر؟ ٥ هَلْ أَنْتَ حَمْدي؟ ٦ مُحَمَّد هُناكَ.

Activity 2

١ أَنا مُحَمَّد. ٢ هِيَ سَحَر. ٣ هَلْ أَنْتَ أَحْمَد؟ ٤ هَلْ أَنْتِ سَحَر؟ ٥ نَحْنُ هُنا.
٦ هَلْ أَنْتُمْ هُنا؟ ٧ هَلْ هُمْ هُناكَ؟ ٨ أَنا حَمْدي وهُوَ أَحْمَد.

Activity 3

١d; ٢k; ٣i; ٤b; ٥h; ٦l; ٧g; ٨c; ٩e; ١٠f; ١١a; ١٢j

Activity 4

١T; ٢F; ٣T; ٤F; ٥F; ٦T

Unit 2

Activity 1

١ هَذا ٢ هَذِهِ ٣ هَذا ٤ هَذا ٥ هَذِهِ ٦ هَذا ٧ هَذِهِ ٨ هَذِهِ

Activity 2

Order of the conversation (from top to bottom).

٢ ← ٣ ← ٦ ← ١ ← ٤ ← ٥

Activity 3

١ ما ٢ أَيْنَ ٣ كَيْفَ ٤ مَنْ ٥ هَلْ ٦ ما

Activity 4

هَذِهِ هِيَ دَرّاجَتي الجَديدة.
اِسْمُها "الريشة". ذَلِكَ لِأَنَّ دَرّاجَتي
سَريعة وَجَميلة وخَفيفة مِثْل الريشة!
هَذِهِ هِيَ قِصّة اِسْم دَرّاجَتي!

Unit 3

Activity 1

١ كَتَبَتْ سَميحة اِسْمها. ٢ هَذا الجَمَل مِن السَّعوديّة. ٣ العُلْبة فَوْقَ المائِدة.
٤ يَجْلِس الكَلْب بَيْنَ الحَقيبَتَيْن. ٥ مَنْ أَكَلَ السَّمَكة؟ ٦ المِفْتاح تَحْتَ الكُرْسيّ.
٧ السَّيّارة عِنْدَ الخَيْمة.

Activity 2

١b; ٢h; ٣f; ٤a; ٥i; ٦c; ٧j; ٨d; ٩e; ١٠g

Activity 3

١ إلى الجامِعة ٢ بالمِتْرو ٣ بَعْدَ الجِسْر ٤ بِجانِب الشُّبّاك ٥ على الهاتِف
٦ فَوْقَ مَكْتَب ٧ قَريب مِن الجامِعة ٨ بالدَّرّاجة ٩ بِدَرّاجَتي السَّريعة

Unit 4

Activity 1

١d; ٢g; ٣a; ٤e; ٥b; ٦c; ٧f

Activity 2

There is a model recording numbered 16 on the audio.

Activity 3

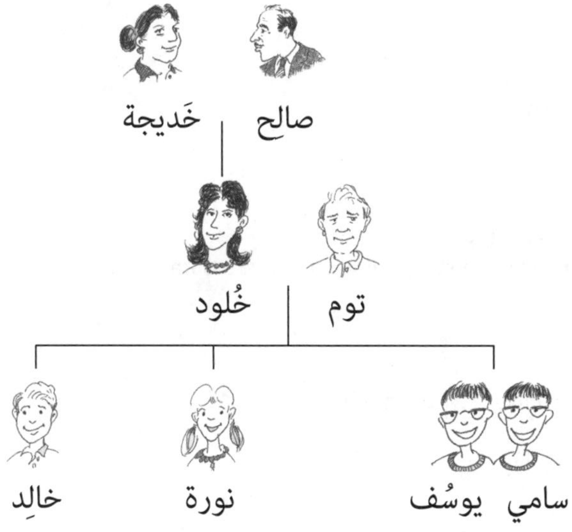

Activity 4

١c; ٢b; ٣a; ٤c; ٥a; ٦a

Activity 5

١ My <u>parents</u> live with my <u>grandmother</u>.
٢ My <u>grandfather</u> said that he goes to the park with his <u>grandchildren</u> every day.
٣ My <u>cousins</u> work together <u>in</u> a carpet factory.
٤ My <u>fiancée</u> and I will visit her <u>family</u> in the village of 'Palace of Palms'.
٥ The life of my <u>(paternal) aunt</u> is hard because she is <u>divorced</u> and her <u>children</u> are young.
٦ My <u>(maternal) uncle</u> paid all the expenses of the wedding of my older <u>sister</u>.

Activity 6

١T; ٢F; ٣T; ٤F; ٥F; ٦F; ٧T; ٨T

Activity 7

There is a model recording numbered 18 on the audio.

Unit 5

Activity 1

١ نَجّار ٢ مُصَوِّر ٣ طَبّاخ ٤ فَنّان ٥ خَبّاز ٦ طَبيب

Activity 2

١b; ٢c; ٣a; ٤a; ٥b; ٦b

Activity 3

مدير/مساعد/مهندسين/مهندسين/عمّال/موظّفين

1 assistant manager and chief engineer
2 a thousand
3 24 hours a day
4 behind the factory
5 in a small palace next to the sea
6 yes, because Mohammed lives next to the sea and (we assume) also near the factory.

Activity 4

There is a model recording numbered 21 on the audio.

Activity 5

١T; ٢F; ٣T; ٤F; ٥T; ٦T

Activity 6

١j (*yaعmal*); ٢d (*ḍaعīfa*); ٣h (*sā'iq*); ٤e (*aعmal*); ٥a (*sharika*); ٦g (*qawīya*); ٧i (*rawātib*); ٨f (*taعmal*); ٩b (*maḥall*); ١٠c (*li-bayع*)

Activity 7

٧:٣٠ ص اجتماع مع المحاسب

٩:٣٠ ص اجتماع مع كلّ المَندوبين

٢:٠٠ م زِيارة المَصنَع الجديد

٥:٠٠ م محلّ الورد

٦:٠٠ م زِيارة مديرة المَبيعات في المستشفى

Activity 8

There is a model recording numbered 24 on the audio.

Unit 6

Activity 1

١ أَريكة ٢ باب ٣ سَجّادة ٤ سَرير ٥ وِسادة ٦ كُرْسيّ

Activity 2

١e; ٢d; ٣f; ٤a; ٥c; ٦b

Activity 3

١ السرير الصغير في الغرفة الصغيرة ٢ الخزانة الكبيرة بجانب الأريكة
٣ الثلّاجة بجانب باب المطبخ ٤ السرير الكبير والكراسي في غرفة النوم
٥ كلّ الوسائد على السرير الكبير ٦ الفرن بين الشبّاك والباب

Activity 4

There is a model recording numbered 27 on the audio.

Activity 5

١f; ٢e; ٣c; ٤a; ٥b; ٦d; ٧g

Activity 6

1T; 2T; 3F; 4T; 5F; 6F

Activity 7

١ سأطير إلى أبها ٢ الفُندُق الفاخِر ٣ أَنْتَقِل من مدينة إلى مدينة ٤ مَندوب مَبيعات
٥ وِسادة سابِعة ٦ كَراسي مُريحة ٧ فوق الباب ٨ ثلّاجة صغيرة

Activity 8

There is a model recording numbered 29 on the audio.

Unit 7

Activity 1

١c; ٢f; ٣e; ٤a; ٥b; ٦d

Activity 2

There is a model recording numbered 32 on the audio.

Activity 3

١a; ٢c; ٣b; ٤a; ٥a; ٦c

Activity 4

أنا اسمي حكيم. أنا سائِق باص. أنا أعرِف كلّ شارع في
هذه المدينة الجميلة، وكلّ مدرسة، وكلّ بيت. في الصباح،
يركَب بَعض الناس الباص، وهو في الموقِف، قَبلَ أن أَخرُج
بِهِ إلى الشوارع. بَعدَ أن نَخرُج من وسط المدينة، وبَعدَ
الجسر الكبير، آخُذ طريق الملك حتّى مَوقِف الجامعة.
ينزل الطَلَبة والمُدَرِّسون هناك. بعد ذلك، آخُذ أوّل شارع
على اليمين، لِآخُذ طريق المطار إلى محطّة المستشفى،
محطّة المُمَرِّضات والمُمَرِّضين!
يَقول كلّ الناس: «شكراً يا عمّ حكيم!» وأنا أقول لَهُمْ،
«مع السلامة يا أَصْدِقائى!»، ثُمَّ أذهب بالباص حتّى المطار.

Activity 5

١T; ٢T; ٣T; ٤F; ٥F; ٦T

Activity 6

1 Khadija Barakat was looking for *The Artists' Restaurant*.
2 She was staying in a hotel called *Palace of the Stars*.
3 First, she asked the boy who operates the elevator.
4 He suggested asking at the post office. 'Take the first street on the left', he said, 'before the square.'
5 So, next Khadija asked the employee at the post office, and he didn't know either.
6 By the end of the story, Khadija had gone a complete circle!

Activity 7

١c; ٢b; ٣b; ٤c; ٥b

Activity 8

There is a model recording numbered 35 on the audio.

Unit 8

Activity 1

١f; ٢e; ٣c; ٤g; ٥h; ٦i; ٧a; ٨d; ٩b

Activity 2

١ يوم الاثنين ٢ ٩,٣٠ صباحاً ٣ يوم السبت ٤ ١٠,١٥ صباحاً ٥ يوم الثلاثاء ٦ ١,٣٠ بعد الظهر

Activity 3

There is a model recording numbered 37 on the audio.

Activity 4

١ أنا طالب في المدرسة الثانوية.
٢ غادَرْتُ المدرسة المتوسّطة السَّنة الماضية.
٣ أنا أُحِبّ أيّام الاثنين.
٤ نحن ندرُس العُلوم في الصباح.
٥ يفضّل ماجد أيّام الثُّلاثاء.
٦ يُحبّ أن يقرأ كُتُب التاريخ.
٧ أريد أن أُسجِّل اِبْنَتي في كُلّيّة الطبّ.
٨ يأمَل ماجِد أن يُسجِّل نَفسَهُ في كُلّيّة الحُقوق.

Activity 5

١ كلّيّة الهندسة ٢ جامعة «وارسو» ٣ الأَساتِذة ٤ كيف تُصنَع الغَسّالات
٥ كيف تعمَل المَصاعِد ٦ مُهندس كبير ومُهِمّ ٧ بسُرعة وبسُهولة ٨ أبناء البَلَد

Activity 6

١F; ٢T; ٣T; ٤F; ٥T; ٦T

Activity 7

There is a model recording numbered 39 on the audio.

Unit 9

Activity 1

١c; ٢c; ٣a; ٤b; ٥c; ٦b

Activity 2

There is a model recording numbered 42 on the audio.

Activity 3

نَحنُ طَلَبة أمريكيّون. نَدرُس التاريخ ونُحِبّ قِراءة الكُتُب القديمة. في الشَّهر الماضي، سافَرْنا إلى القاهرة في مصر، ونَزِلْنا في فُندُق كبير أمام الأهرام. بَعدَ ذلك، زُرْنا أسوان في الجَنوب، ثُمَّ أَخَذْنا المَركَب إلى الشَّمال لنَذهَب إلى الأُقصُر. في البَرّ الغَربيّ من النَّهر، جَلَسْنا بجانِب مَعْبَد فِرْعونيّ، وتَكَلَّمَ الأساتِذة عَن وادي المُلوك، وعَن طيبة وهي العاصِمة القديمة. بَعدَ ذلك أَخَذْنا الطائرة وسافَرْنا إلى الأُردُنّ. هناك، زُرْنا مدينة عَمّان، ووادي رُم والبَتراء. نحن تَعَلَّمْنا الكثير في هذه الرِّحْلة، وسَنَرجِع إلى الشَّرْق الأَوْسط في السنة القادمة وسَنَزور بِلاداً أُخرى!

Activity 4

1F; 2T; 3F; 4F; 5T; 6F; 7T

Activity 5

١ جنسيّة ٢ تأشيرات ٣ سفارات ٤ مُدير ٥ موظّفون ٦ وُصول ٧ غَرب أوروبا
٨ شَمال إفريقيا ٩ واحدة من ١٠ عَواصِم ١١ مَطلوب ١٢ روما

Activity 6

١b; ٢c; ٣c; ٤a; ٥b

Activity 7

There is a model recording numbered 45 on the audio.

Unit 10

Activity 1

١c; ٢g; ٣b; ٤h; ٥d; ٦a; ٧f; ٨e

Activity 2

١ يوم السَّبت هو يوم السوق في قَرْيَتنا.
٢ اِشْتَرَتْ أختي كيمونو ليمونيّ مَصنوع من الحرير.
٣ سَتَبْحَث خالَتي عن مائدة مَصنوعة من الخشب.
٤ سَتَشْتَري أمّي حقيبة رَماديّة يوم السبت القادِم.
٥ تاجِر الكيمونو من الصين.
يَبيع الكيمونو بِألوان ومقاسات كثيرة.
٦ في السوق، اشتَرَيْتُ خاتِمي المَصنوع من الذَّهَب.

Activity 3
There is a model recording numbered 48 on the audio.

Activity 4
١f; ٢h; ٣a; ٤d; ٥b; ٦g; ٧c; ٨e

Activity 5
1 Tuesday.
2 A green cotton hat.
3 It hasn't arrived yet.
4 Yes, he has.
5 Basket number 88T, dated Monday.
6 To go and have breakfast. The delivery is on its way.

Activity 6
١c; ٢a; ٣c; ٤b; ٥b; ٦a; ٧b; ٨b

Activity 7
There is a model recording numbered 51 on the audio.

Unit 11

Activity 1
١b; ٢c; ٣a; ٤c; ٥b; ٦a; ٧c; ٨b

Activity 2
١d; ٢c; ٣b; ٤f; ٥h; ٦g; ٧e; ٨a

Activity 3
١ اِشتَرَيتُ هذا الخبز من المخبز.
٢ هذه قَهوَتي. سَأَشْرَبُها الآن.
٣ هَل اِشتَرَيتَ هذه الخضروات من الخُضَريّ.
٤ شَرِبنا عصير الفواكه في هذا المحلّ.
٥ اِشْتَرَيتُ هذا السمك من السمّاك.
٦ دَفَعوا هذا الحساب لصاحِبة المحلّ.
٧ اِشْتَرَتْ أمّي هذا الشاي من البقّالة.
٨ اِشْتَرى أبي هذه الدجاجة من اللحّام.

Activity 4
There is a model recording numbered 53 on the audio.

Activity 5

البقّالة	الخضريّ	السمّاك	اللحّام
فِلفِل أسود (black pepper)	بطاطس (potatoes)	٦ سمكات (6 fish)	٦ دجاجات (6 chickens)
أرزّ (rice)	ثوم (garlic)	جَمبَريّ (prawns)	لحم مفروم (minced meat)
جُبن (cheese)	بصل أحمر (red onions)		
زيت (oil)	ورق عنب (vine leaves)		
حمّص (chick peas)	باذنجان (aubergines)		
زيتون (olives)	طماطم (tomatoes)		
خَلّ (vinegar)	خيار (cucumber)		
زبيب (raisins)	ليمون (lemons)		
زبادي (yoghurt)	جزر (carrots)		
	گرفس (celery)		
	نَعناع (mint)		

Activity 6

١ أتناول إفطاري ٢ واقِفاً ٣ جالِساً على مكتبي ٤ أما عشائي ٥ وَجبة جاهِزة
٦ آكُلها في البيت ٧ المصنوعة من البوليستيرين ٨ مصنوعة من البلاستك

Activity 7

There is a model recording numbered 56 on the audio.

Unit 12

Activity 1

١a; ٢c; ٣c; ٤b; ٥c; ٦a; ٧b

Activity 2

There is a model recording numbered 58 on the audio.

Activity 3

Shukri: I'm Egyptian. I work in a large museum. My name is Shukri.
Zahra: And I'm Zahra. I'm an actress in the theatre.
Shukri: One rainy morning, I met Zahra on the steps of the theatre.
Zahra: I was walking quickly towards the door and he was with his dog, Tito.

Shukri: I said to her: "Why are you walking quickly when the weather is rainy and the water is everywhere?!".

Zahra: I said to him: "Firstly, let's get aquainted! What's the name of ... this beautiful dog?".

Shukri: We laughed, and after that we became friends, me and her and Tito!

Zahra: We both enjoyed walking in the parks and watching films in the cinema.

Shukri: And finally, we got married twenty years ago.

Activity 4

١ *(to swim)* **f** *(swimming)*; ٢ *(to meet)* **i** *(meeting)*; ٣ *(to head [for])* **j** *(heading [for])*;

٤ *(to drive/to lead)* **a** *(driving/leading)*; ٥ *(to enjoy)* **h** *(enjoyment)*;

٦ *(to watch)* **c** *(watching)*; ٧ *(to smell)* **e** *(smelling)*; ٨ *(to reserve)* **b** *(reservation)*;

٩ *(to visit)* **d** *(visiting)*; ١٠ *(to laugh)* **g** *(laughing)*

Activity 5

1 Always pleasant and sunny.
2 No, he doesn't. (He likes to stay in his country.)
3 To smell the sea breeze and swim in the [resort of] Binzert.
4 To meet Tunisians and to walk amongst them to see their natural [way of] life.
5 To visit the oases and enjoy seeing the palm trees.
6 The old forts.

Activity 6

There is a model recording numbered 61 on the audio.

Unit 13

Activity 1

١b; ٢c; ٣b; ٤c; ٥b; ٦c; ٧a; ٨a; ٩c

Activity 2

١ كلّ يوم، أَصْحو الساعة السابعة والنصف.
٢ بَعدَ ذلك أغسِل وَجهي.
٣ أنظُر من الشبّاك لِأرى حالة الطقس.
٤ عادةً أتَناوَل إفطاري الساعة الثامنة.
٥ أحياناً ألعَب بَعضَ الرياضة الخفيفة.
٦ أخرُج من البيت الساعة التاسعة والربع.

Activity 3

There is a model recording numbered 64 on the audio.

Activity 4

١ أتوجّه نحو ٢ شبّاك الحمّام ٣ حالة الطَّقس ٤ كوب الشاي الأوَّل
٥ أُفَكِّر في إفطاري ٦ أي طعام يُقابِلني ٧ إذا كانَ ٨ بَيضة مَسلوقة

Activity 5

1F; 2F; 3T; 4F; 5F; 6T; 7T; 8F

Activity 6

There is an open-ended writing activity. The commentary will depend on your own evening routine. Try to show your finished piece to an Arabic speaker.

Unit 14

Activity 1

١ *(king)* **c** *(kings)*; ٢ *(government)* **f** *(governments)*; ٣ *(minister)* **e** *(ministers)*;
٤ *(feast/festival)* **h** *(feasts/festivals)*; ٥ *(people/populace)* **g** *(peoples/populaces)*;
٦ *(industry)* **a** *(industries)*; ٧ *(religion)* **b** *(religions)*; ٨ *(society)* **d** *(societies)*

Activity 2

There is a model recording numbered 67 on the audio.

Activity 3

1 the economy
2 public holiday
3 visiting dignitaries
4 general inspiration

Activity 4

1 Special thanks to the Minister of the Economy who has helped me. Our economy is strong and is growing every day!
2 Happy Eid/feast on the occasion of National Day. Health and happiness to all the people!
3 I received a group of princes today. The future is bright for everyone!
4 The government is working for you seven days a week. Together we will build a better life!

Activity 5

١ قانونيّ ٢ اِقتِصاديّ ٣ ثَقافيّ ٤ دينيّ ٥ صِناعيّ
٦ تَقليديّ ٧ شَعبيّ ٨ صِحّيّ ٩ عَقليّ

Activity 6

Messages 1, 3 and 5.

Activity 7

١b; ٢c; ٣c; ٤a; ٥b; ٦a

Activity 8

This is an open-ended writing activity. The slogans and posters will depend on your imagination and preferences. Try to show your finished piece to an Arabic speaker.